THE
FACTS
OF
LIFE

THE
FACTS
OF
LIFE

RAGHAVENDRA BHAT

PARTRIDGE
A Penguin Random House Company

To order additional copies of this book, contact
Partridge India
000 800 10062 62
orders.india@partridgepublishing.com

www.partridgepublishing.com/india

CONTENTS

MY NEW FRIEND - A SPECIAL CROW

I am a consultant physician - I teach at a medical college where I head the department of Medicine. I also practice in a first floor clinic which also has a balcony. Traditionally we keep some water for crows in a mug. Unlike in the past when many crows used to frequent it, nowadays, a few crows only come signifying a dwindling population of crows.

One day, I observed that the mug had fallen down and the water had spilled. I was curious to know why. There was no ready explanation visible. I saw the same thing happen next day. My curiosity was aroused. Crows do not waste water normally. I waited for a while looking around. Then I refilled the mug with water and waited. A crow came by and pushed the mug spilling the water - it was an incredible sight. My first instinct was to shoo it away but I observed something unusual - the crow just sat there looking at me. I gave it a prolonged look more out of contempt for the crow being "naughty" and suddenly observed something

1

unusual - its upper beak was only half the size of the lower beak (which was normal) which meant that there was no suction effect - it could not suck water out of mug which is narrow and long. I realized that it needed a shallow, open container.

Next day, I replaced the mug with a wide container and waited for the crow. Sure enough he came. He promptly started looking at me and crowing. Not knowing how to respond, I spoke to him in my mother tongue and encouraged him to drink water. After 5 minutes of incessant crowing, he dipped himself into the container of water, had a nice bath and then proceeded to drink water to his heart's content. After he had his fill, he came out sat next to me at a point blank range and crowed continuously- probably its way of thanking me.

The whole episode was a revealing experience for me - For one thing, the communication skill of the crow - It never had any formal training or a degree in communication and yet it could very effectively communicate with me and educate me about its problem. I do not think a trained person could have done better under the circumstances. The other thing I observed was its gratitude. Even now, he comes every day, has his bath, drinks water and communicates with me by crowing. If I am working inside, he patiently waits and only after I come out and talk to him will he drink water. Only after thanking me he will leave. He makes it a point to call many other crows too! When such qualities of leadership, communication skills and gratitude are observed in a simple crow, what is happening to the educated humans?

WHY DO WE FAIL TO CONTROL MALARIA?

Malaria is an ancient disease. It is a shame that Malaria still kills and kills more people than AIDS does. It is a disease produced by the malarial parasite (a unicellular organism), which should by sheer chance find a female anopheles mosquito at the right time for its very survival. This mosquito thus infected (vector) has to bite a human being at the appropriate time to inject the half developed malarial parasite into the blood of a human being so that the development is continued. There is no need to overemphasize the "strength" of the parasite as we are well aware that the infections mainly by the Plasmodium falciparum can be lethal because of damage to multiple organs (kidney, brain, liver being the commonest).

Don't we have medicines strong enough? We do! Don't we have government support? We do! Then what is the problem? Why are we failing? Well I am ashamed to tell you why. As you have rightly understood, this disease can

3

be compared to a chain with 3 links - the malarial parasite at the bottom of the evolutionary scale; the female anopheles mosquito a little above that with some independent abilities but still needing sheer chance to come into contact with 2 different species at the right time for continuation of the cycle; and the human being on the highest scale of evolution who has tremendous knowledge and intelligence and can work wonders if he wants to. But there is a strange fallacy - these two "lowly evolved" species work single mindedly for their survival while the human being overwhelmed by greed works at cross purposes mainly to undermine and destroy others of his own species. New constructions have boomed everywhere. Cheap labor is imported who also have untreated or partly treated malaria. Treating them would cost very little to the builder but is never done (and they have the malarial parasite in their blood always). Water is added and kept for curing of the concrete which provides ideal conditions for mosquito breeding. Adding guppy fish will control this but is never done (basically shows the mentality of the builders). Naturally malaria is rampant around new construction sites. No wonder then the maximum attacks and repeat attacks are found in construction industry. Now you know one of the reasons why malaria is not being controlled.

The other important reason is that we have evolved backward in our civic sense while we progressed forward economically. We get a pleasure out of throwing garbage into our neighborhood - in fact anywhere as long as it is outside our compound! Also drugs are not taken properly by the patients - self (mis)treatment is rampant. Chemist assisted mistreatment is more dangerous. Non- reporting of the cases denies opportunity for a proper control. If we humans do not mend our ways, forget about eliminating malaria, the parasite will one day succeed in eliminating human race! Let us wake up to hard facts. It is still not too late!

THE TELEPHONE ETIQUETTE

I distinctly remember the day telephone came home for the first time. It made personal contact much easier. My dad, a busy doctor, much to the happiness of his patients, became easily accessible. He was a stickler for time and therefore his movements to the clinic and home were highly predictable making it easy to contact him. We had to take his permission to use it. It would be at a time when he did not expect calls. The duration of conversation had to be brief and to the point - it was a doctor's phone.

There was a method in using the phone. On lifting the receiver, a lady's voice would say "Number please". We would give the number and wait. She would connect us and then say "speak on". We would hear the voice on the other side say "Hello" and start speaking. The whole activity was cordial and pleasurable. Of course, "wrong number" was an interesting offshoot. It sometimes connected us really to the wrong people resulting in unintentional humour. "Where is the masala dosa I asked for an hour ago?" screamed a man. He was not believing it was a wrong number. I had to convince him that the said dosa will arrive in next 30 minutes that he disconnected. Without both parties disconnecting it was not possible to make a fresh call. Sometimes in times of distress, the "Wrong number" would help one to get out of the tight spot.

Many years later the gruff looking black telephone gave way to a cute red set "Indira Priyadarshini" more of a showpiece but well loved. It was not permissible to keep 2 sets in parallel connection. Dad used to sleep upstairs and the phone was in the drawing room downstairs. We had a bell upstairs which would ring along with the phone downstairs and he had to rapidly walk down the staircase within 10 rings at dead of the night to successfully take the call. Trunk calls were a different ball game. One would book a trunk call and wait almost endlessly. It would magically ring when you almost gave up! The conversation had t be really rapid to be over in 3 minutes because then it would be spill over to a second call.

All this changed drastically with the advent of the mobile phones. Ease of communication increased. It was easy to call anybody anytime. Anytime became telephone time. There was an invasion into privacy. Courtesy vanished. No "number please" or "Hello". Conversation started even before the receiver understood what was happening! We learnt to spend minutes and then hours on the phone ignoring important activities.

From a facilitator of communication, phones are becoming a menace. There in less fun and enjoyment in calls particularly when you are otherwise occupied. Calling a girl / boy friend has become easy but avoiding one has become difficult!

No doubt this instrument (mobile phone) is an innovative product. We have innovated even further. We have created a special calling system - "Missed call" at NO COST whatsoever to the user! It gives an indication who is calling. It is sometimes used as a code for an answer (a missed call may mean yes). The million dollar question, however, remains, do we really need such instant connectivity all the time?

THE HISTORIC LANDMARK - GOVERNMENT WENLOCK HOSPITAL

I do not think there is anyone who has some knowledge of Mangalore who does not know Government Wenlock Hospital. Standing majestically at the very heart of the city it has been a witness to the evolution of medical treatment and later medical education in Mangalore. It started in 1848 by the East India Company on the request of the public of Mangalore. in a small old building near the present location of Lady Goschen Hospital. In 1861, people decided to collect money and run their own hospital themselves because they liked it very much! Many illustrious doctors served here. Sir Ronald Ross, who was awarded the Nobel prize for his historic work in proving the role of mosquitoes in the transmission of Malaria worked here in the late 18 hundreds. Lt. Col Charles Donovan served as the DMO of the hospital from 1895 - 1897. He became famous for his discovery of the causative organism

(Donovan bodies)of then dreaded disease Kala Azar. In 1871, the city administration took over the hospital. In 1919 Madras Presidency took over the hospital. This was relocated in the new building at the current location. The foundation stone was laid by Lord Wenlock who was then the Governor of Madras province. The hospital was later named after him.

The further developments naturally followed. Janghan, a trader from Hong Kong donated Rs. 500 for starting the operation theatres in 1903. In 1938, Kudpi Bhujanga Rao of Bombay donated the first ambulance to the hospital fulfilling the long felt need of the public. 1920 s and 30 s saw rapid strides of development with addition of new wards and amalgamation of the Police hospital. In 1955, Kasturba Medical College got formal attachment to this hospital for training the medical students - an unique landmark public private partnership in the post independent era due to the visionary Dr. TMA Pai. The public of Mangalore and neighbouring districts and states immensely benefitted from this. Expert doctors were (and still are) available for consultation for the common man free. What followed was truly the golden era of the Wenlock Hospital. The first heart surgery in the Karnataka State in the Government sector took place here on 13 February 1975 by Dr. SR Ullal. People of Mangalore thronged the place for the best services - I remember my own mother getting successfully operated there in 1964 for a complex kidney problem! The hospital has been greatly helped and supported by private organisations like Mangalore Medical Relief society(ICU, Cardiac ward); Lions Clubs((Artificial Limbs centre, Paediatric ward, Renal Dialysis ward, Burns ward, Neonatal ward); Rotary Club (Physiotherapy); Infosys(RAPCC - Speciality Paediatric

Hospital). Innumerable personal beneficiaries and small organizations including youth clubs have supported various projects from time to time.

Currently the hospital caters to 7 districts from 3 states. Latest statistics include a bed strength of 705. In 2013, 7051 in patients and 85730 outpatients were treated ; 3659 Dialysis sessions were conducted; 5393 Major and 1734 Minor surgeries including 999 cataract surgeries took place. A selfless, dedicated team of doctors, nurses, paramedical and support staff serve there in close coordination and harmony with an efficient team of government doctors and the other government staff. The interest taken by the KMC is reflected in the prompt service and the efficient role of the government is visible in the clean and efficient administration headed by the district surgeon ably supported by her team.

Remember, Wenlock Hospital is your hospital. At least visit it once. You will be overwhelmed. Donate something if you feel like helping the poor public. If not at least get awed by the great monument that has stood the test of time and is still working efficiently! If you let me know in advance, you can meet me and my efficient and compassionate team of doctors there!

THE STORY OF CHLOROQUINE IN MALARIA

Malaria is an ancient foe. A real killer - it kills more patients than AIDS does. The story of rise and fall of Malaria has closely followed human greed - more attacks and deaths during war and less during peace times. It has also paralleled the human behaviour and civic sense - poor civic sense has always been an permanent invitation to Malaria. And poor civic sense does not necessarily go and in hand with poverty. Builders are a case in point - they hire poor laborers always harboring the parasites and water left (open) for curing make a deadly combination and help in sustaining and spreading malaria.

Around the second world war, there was rapid spread of malaria. An urgent need was felt to discover new and effective and safe drugs safer than then available Quinine which produced deafness on long term use. Research in the Veterans Armed Forces Hospital yielded 3 new drugs - Chloroquine, Mefloquine and Amodiaquine of which Chloroquine was the best tolerated. Naturally it started becoming popular.

This was a German discovery by a pharmaceutical company Bayer and Hitler got wind of it. He realized the potential and banned the drug from reaching the Allies - the French, Americans and the British to prove German supremacy. He is even believed to have dropped planeloads of mosquitoes possibly infested (containing malarial parasites) on the allied nations so that he can win the war at least by default (by spreading malaria and making chloroquine unavailable). Needless to say this foolish idea perished with the defeat of Germany. America took this very seriously and in an unusual move, nationalized all holdings of the German pharmaceutical company responsible for the discovery of Chloroquine and auctioned all their land holdings which was bought by Ames a company then making dipsticks thereby demonstrating American supremacy. The Bayer company rightly protested and got rights of continuation of sales in USA through local companies like Glaxo and Roche.

Bayer scientists worked hard and discovered some winner molecules which included Ciprofloxacin and Nifedipine among others These were global hits and the Bayer company bought every inch of the land back and continued to make dipsticks and embossed Bayer on top of Ames to affirm American supremacy. Much later, after many years of use and misuse, we started finding chloroquine resistance, the other drugs - Mefloquine and Amodiaquine were brought out giving an impression that these are new drugs. However, Artisunates were introduced later in the treatment of Malaria which are still useful. Before you go with an idea that these are newest drugs, I will tell you that these were in use in ancient China as Quingashu and was extensively used in the treatment of Malaria.

This brings us to the lesson for the day - it is more important to live better by respecting nature and rediscovering our lost civic sense. We cannot control Malaria without helping nature to control it. We cannot declare war on the nature with senseless deforestation and greedy builders constructing new buildings without proper antimalarial measures. I only hope we change for the better and work towards reducing the incidence of Malaria than trying to discover new drugs which is next to impossible!

SOME MORE FACTS ABOUT THE HISTORIC LANDMARK - GOVERNMENT WENLOK HOSPITAL

I am overwhelmed by the response for the blog on Government Wenlock Hospital. It is indeed a landmark in the city of Mangalore. It started functioning in 1848 - I gave it as oversight as 1948 - vigilant readers(DR. Ashok Kumar was the first one) have corrected me. I am grateful to them. The date is significant because only a few hospitals and medical colleges started before that in India (Madras General Hospital in 1772, Calcutta Medical school in 1824, Grant Medical college in 1843). That was also the year of "gold rush" where people rushed to to California. People of Mangalore valued the hospital as much as gold!

The public of Mangalore were desperate to have a hospital for themselves in Mangalore and therefore submitted a memorandum to the government. In response, the East India Company board of directors issued an order to start a Military

Hospital in Mangalore in 1848. It was located in the place where the Lady Goschen Hospital is now situated. This was a rented building with a monthly rent of Rs. 14. This is the list of the limited staff and the salaries paid to them --- A doctor (Rs. 50 / month); a dresser (Rs. 24); a cook (Rs. 7); a peon (Rs. 4 and 8 annas); a scavenger (Rs. 3 and 8 annas); a watchman (Rs. 5). A year later, the IP were 45 and OP were 1447 (in 1849). In 1851, it was shifted to its own building. The first local surgeon was appointed in 1852. (whose salary was Rs. 100) who would treat people and help the district surgeon. In 1861, the people of Mangalore decided not to take help from the government and to run the hospital on their own with the local donations!In 1861, the local administration took over the hospital and ran it. In 1871, 165 IP s and 3898 OP s were treated. 1870 s saw people accepting the "hospital culture". New hospitals were started in Puttur (1872), Udupi (1887) and Karkal (1890). In 1893, the then Governor Lord Wenlock visited the hospital and Dr. Bannerman was the medical officer. In 1919, the Madras Presidency took over all the hospitals. A new building was constructed at the present location and the hospital was shifted there and it was named after then Governor, Lord Wenlock.

In 1903 Janghen, a trade from Hong Kong visited Mangalore was impressed and donated Rs. 500 for the Operation Theatre Complex. The ambulance, a long felt need was fulfilled by Kudpi Bhujanga Rao from Bombay. In 1920 s and 30 s new wards were started and the Police hospital was amalgamated. 1948 saw a double celebration for Mangaloreans - Hundredth anniversary of the Wenlock hospital and first anniversary of Independence. The it had 110 beds.

1955 saw a great PPP (public private partnership) of post independence era take place in the form of KMC joining hands with the government in running the hospital and permission for its use in teaching medical students. This was possible due largely to the vision of Dr. TMA Pai, the founder of Kasturba Medical College. What followed was truly a golden era - a unique win - win situation for the government, the public and the medical students and the medical college benefitted. The specialities started around 1955. The hospital was extended with the addition of speciality wards around 1963 - the foundation stone was laid by then CM Veerendra Patil who through the government donated a sum of Rs. 9 lakhs. In 1966, 613 IP s and 1086 OP s were treated. Private sector contributed to its development in a big way- Mangalore Medical Relief Society donated ICU and Cardiac ward. Lions International donated Artificial limbs centre, Pediatric ward, Dialysis unit, Burns ward, Neonatal ward. Rotary donated the Physiotherapy centre. Infosys donated the state of the art Paediatric care facility RAPCC. Specialized machines followed - CT scan, Endoscope, Laproscope became available to the common man. Today in its 167 th year of its existence, this landmark hospital is proudly serving many districts of Karnataka (South Kanara, Udupi, North Kanara, Hassan, Coorg, Chickamangalur, and also some of the neighbouring states of Kerala, Tamil Nadu and Andhra Pradesh. Good service despite resource crunch has been the hallmark of this hospital. Thanks to dedicated service from the doctors(KMC as well as the Government doctors), nurses, paramedical and administrative staff the hospital has succeeded in delivering what is expected of it. Long live Wenlock Hospital!

THE IMPORTANCE OF HISTORY TAKING IN PATIENT CARE

Basically I am a clinician which means that I treat patients. History taking is an important part of the clinical analysis of the patient. There was a time this was being done diligently - maybe history taking and clinical examinations were the only 2 skills available to the doctors then. Of course some simple blood and urine tests were possible and were being done if needed. This assured that adequate time was spent by the doctor with the patient giving scope for a good communication, observation and documentation which forms the basis of a good logical diagnosis. A correct diagnosis is essential for proper management of the patient and best results.

This brings us back to history taking - how important is it in this modern era of advanced technology? Is it not enough if a trained (not necessarily a doctor) person takes the data on a ticking basis saving time for the doctor? Sadly,

NO. It is interesting to note that 80 - 90 per cent of the times the diagnosis is made by history and good clinical examination. All the new technology and the machines only help in refining further 5 - 10 percent! Face to face interaction, eye contact, listening to the patient, physical examination by the doctor (the doctor's touch) are all important.

The case in point is a patient I saw on last Sunday. I was requested to see a "restless" patient on the Sunday evening. Restlessness would basically point to a problem in the heart / lung / liver / blood sugar related / nervous system related issues / alcohol withdrawal are main causes. The patient was confused and restless. On a detailed history taking from the wife and a diligent clinical examination I drew a blank. Then we do some basic investigations - a chest x ray failed to explain the restlessness. The blood sugar was normal. The ECG taken on modern machine was reported by the machine as "Abnormal - Suggests heart attack" pressing the panic button among the staff and the relatives. This is a bane of modern technology - report comes even if you do not ask for it! Actually, due to confusion and restlessness, the patient was randomly moving his fingers and hand resulting in random "elevation of ST segment and inversion of T waves" which technically amount to a heart attack. In a true heart attack, these changes are seen in all complexes in a given lead always whereas in a patient (like this) with movements, the changes are randomly seen in some complexes sometimes - this is made out only if the doctor observes during the ECG recording or records it himself. There were no abnormalities in the other systems mentioned above. He had not consumed alcohol of late.

The doctor sometimes has to become a detective. Time had come for that. I had overlooked something for sure. No excuse was good enough for that. I had to make amends and find out the truth. I called his wife again. I asked about recent behavioral change - sure enough he was doing double duty indicating manic phase of manic depressive psychosis. Then I asked about "daily medicines" that he takes - the wife suddenly remembered - she brought a strip of Alprazolam (a benzodiazepine drug working on the brain) which he was consuming more than 15 per day - which she believed was a tonic - obviously he was addicted to Alprazolam. He had stopped it suddenly - being accustomed to a continuous intake, it resulted in withdrawal features of which confusion, restlessness and abnormal movements are dominant. He had all of these and a correct diagnosis was made by talking to the patient's relatives. This re emphasis the need for talking to the patient and his family and making sure we are not misled by the advanced machines. We should not be the slave of technology - we should be the masters controlling the technology to our benefit and using it judiciously!

EPONYMS IN MEDICINE

 ${E}_{ponyms}$(Gk. word Epi = upon; onyma = name) are names derived from the names of things diseases/ conditions etc. derived from the name of persons / place / things. We use eponyms in our day to day life without realizing it - Diesel engine (named after Rudolf Diesel), atlas are good examples. Some eponyms come from Mythology - Ulysses syndrome is an example. This reflects unnecessary multiple tests done on patients based on a single abnormal result much like the futility of the tasks done by the mythological Ulysses. Some eponyms are derived from the literature - Pickwickian syndrome (from the fat boy in Picwick papers by Charles Dickens); Jekyll and Hyde syndrome consisting of behaviour disorder with multiple personalities mimiking the character from RL Stevenson's story. Framingham study is a geographic eponym. Legionnaire's disease is a corporate eponym. Many eponyms are named after the discoverer - Quick test after the haematologist and Bowmann's capsule after the anatomist. Some eponyms are attributed to the wrong people - Saint after whom the Saint's triad is named (gall stones, diverticulitis, hiatus hernia) never described it! Some eponyms are shorter and more comfortable than the original disease - Paget's disease is better than the official name osteodystrophica chronica deformans hypertrophica. Eponyms liven the medical history and are said to be "one of the vestiges of the humanism remaining in an increasingly numeralised and computerised society."!

Sometimes more than one eponym describes a single condition - Weil's disease, Fiedler's disease, Landouzy's disease' are the same condition! Sometimes same name denotes different diseases - Pott's fracture, Pott's gangrene, Pott's paralysis, Pott's puffy tumour are different disorders. There are at least 3 different types of Albright syndrome. Some double barrel eponyms exist - Chidiak - Higashi syndrome (hyphenated) was described by 2 people ; Austin Flint murmur (unhyphenaed) is one person! So are the other unhyphenated double eponyms indicating a single person - Marcus Gunn pupil, Ramsay Hunt syndrome, and Bence Jones protein. Lawrence - Moon - Biedl syndrome is a triple eponym which became famous only after Biedl described it. Charcot - Marie - Tooth - Hoffman syndrome is an example of a quadruple eponym.

Tashima syndrome is an interesting one where the physician searches for a new disease to attach his name to. Tashima from Houston described it first. Stingler's law says that many times the eponyms are not named after the original discoverer. Stingler feels that eponymy is the rightful reward of the original discoverer. Pott's fracture was not only described by Pott but also suffered by him.

There is a recent move to drop the apostrophe form possessive eponmys (that is with an apostrophe) so that what was called Hodgkin's disease will now be called Hodgkin disease. Bell palsy (named after Sir Charles Bell) is another example. Sometimes the word "of" is used - Circle of Willis is an example. Saying a positive Babinski (instead of an extensor plantar) is a truncated eponym. To say "to Kocherize" is an example of a derivative eponym. Some eponyms are derived not from people but from things (caisson disease - caisson is a pressurised chamber). Some multiple different eponyms relate to different people - Pick disease (by a German Pathologist); Pick disease (by a Czetch Psychiatrist), Pick Pericarditis (by a Czetch - Austrian physician). Some eponyms have difficult spellings - Kupffer cell, Kuntscher nail, Papanicaolaou smear are some examples.

Whatever it is, doubtlessly the eponyms add life to otherwise dull matters and makes learning interesting. Only time will tell whether the eponyms will withstand the modern methods of learning and teaching!

CASE OF THE "PULSELESS" ASTROLOGER - A TRUE HUMAN INTEREST STORY

I grew up in Mangalore and continue to reside in the same locality. The immediate neighbors have remained the same and we have very cordial working relationship. Each one knows the others. We interact frequently. We help each other.

One day, as I was looking out of the window, I found the old man in the opposite house suddenly fall down to the ground in the compound and get "fits" (convulsions). He had turned blue both the things indicating insufficient blood supply because the heart was beating very slowly. Pulse rate was very slow - around 30 per minute. This is known as Stokes - Adams attack (due to- complete heart block a problem of conduction of the originated heart beat down as the pulse)- a medical emergency. The treatment would entail insertion of a pacemaker after complete check up and treating the cause like a heart attack if there is one. I was very well aware of the social limitations of this patient. Lifelong he was practicing astrology as a hobby without charging anything to the people. Naturally he would not be able to afford a modern life saving gadget costing around Rs. 1,50,000 then. He was honest and self respecting man staying with his daughter, son in law and grand children would never ask others for help. There was no heart attack and it was worth helping him as the rhythm disorder (complete heart block was the only problem) and he really needed the pacemaker fast. He however categorically told me that the pacemaker insertion according to his astrological predictions was possible only after 3 weeks if at all it was done!

What was the alternative? I was in a dilemma. Can such an honest person be left alone because he cannot afford the luxury? My first instinct was to help him. I was figuring out how to. Suddenly I remembered an episode. We had inserted a pacemaker in a patient with OSA (Obstructive Sleep Apnea who had blackouts due to periodic inability of the atria to beat (atrial standstill). When she died, I had requested her son to pull out the pacemaker carefully before the final rites. I phone him hoping it had been done and was glad to know it had indeed been done. I requested him to get the pacemaker. There are issues with reusing the pacemaker- it should be functioning. There is a lead through which the wires thinner than the hair have to pass, This lead was bent and cut! However, I requested my friend, Dr. Mukund, a cardiologist, to try and use this pacemaker. The cardiologist understood the situation and cooperated. On testing the continuity of conduction on the table we were pleasantly happy to observe that the pacemaker was nicely functional despite the lead being cut and bent! A miracle indeed! After all the pacemaker was in use only intermittently for less than 2 years in the earlier patient and the lithium battery should usually last for around 10 years. Anyway, the pacemaker was working well and there was no reason why it should not work for long! I checked the date - it was exactly 3 weeks after the first episode of fall! It took so much time to arrange the pacemaker and then the cardiologist had to go out of station for a few days. His prediction had come true!

It was a very satisfying experience for all of us! WE could help a genuinely needy person for the fraction of the cost (entire cost came to about Rs. 15'000 instead of Rs. 1,50,000. What really made me happy was the observation that many people some unknown to him willingly helped him. The episode re imposed my faith in my firm belief - "the society will always pay its rightful due to the deserving person" - only I wish to see this happen more often! He lived happily for 8 more years and continued his hobby of free astrology consultations all along!

THE STORY OF HOW ANTI TUBERCULAR TREATMENT STARTED IN MANGALORE

Today I am going to tell you a story - the story of how anti-tubercular treatment evolved with special reference to Mangalore. You may wonder how am I authorised to tell the story -in fact, my father (late Dr. VR Bhat) is the one who started the anti tubercular treatment in Mangalore. He started his practice at Chitra Clinic in 1947 and as he was specially trained (at Madras) in handling tuberculosis, his patients mostly were suffering from tuberculosis / its / complications / sequellae /mimics like bronchiectasis. At that time tuberculosis was a dreaded killer. We (my sister and me) watched it from close quarters. Both of us saw dad work hard and save lives. Treatment was very little in the beginning when no specific anti TB drugs were available - the concept was to give good food and rest to the lungs and offer them good ventilation and fresh air. Sanatorium treatment fitted the bill very well.

The worst patients were referred to Perandurai sanatorium at Madras. Artificial pneumothorax to intentionally collapse the lung harboring the lesion having caused life threatening haemoptysis was another modality of treatment which needed immense skill so that air embolism a dreaded complication had to be avoided.

Almost at that time Injectable Streptomycin became available. Each injection of 1 gram would cost more than a couple of sovereigns of gold! At Rs. 32 it was an expensive lifesaver if the patient lived long enough. The trouble was to get Streptomycin. Being expensive, no chemist would touch it. It had to be imported from London, bought at Madras by paying cash and then transported to Mangalore by train in a cold chain (in ice as was the custom then) and stored in a refrigerator. Refrigerators were hardly available in Mangalore. My dad felt that the facilities for these patients must be provided in one place and therefore, he provided Chest X Rays, facilities for blood counts, for sputum AFB testing all in his Chitra Clinic where he did all of these himself for reasons of accuracy and privacy. After procuring the Streptomycin, it would be stored in a fridge at the Sri Ramakrishna Ashram where one of the swamiji was his close friend.

Imagine the scenario which was common and which we (the family) witnessed almost every night. A patient would have haemoptysis and one of the relatives would rush to our house. Dad would ask his address, and ask him to go home. Then he would wake up our next door neighbour - his man Friday for such occasions. Both would go in my dad's Morris minor car and reach the side of the road outside the window of the room in the Sri Ramakrishna Ashram where the swamiji slept. They would throw a stone at the window pane with just enough impact to wake up the swamiji without breaking the glass pane. The swamiji would come out with 1 injection of Streptomycin. Armed with that and other paraphernalia (a BP apparatus, a stethoscope, sterilised glass syringe, cotton, spirit etc in a handsome Doctor's bag) they would reach the patient's house, examine him reassure him, start Inj Streptomycin and other available treatment. Next day he would be evaluated at the clinic for the proper diagnosis. The best part was the charges levied to the patient - Streptomycin would be passed on at no extra cost. Many patients being poor failed to pay even that partially or completely - dad just forgot and forgave them and moved ahead. The consultation, chest x ray, blood and sputum tests would cost the patient Rs. 30 (a little more than the actual cost price)!Naturally, we had to get a merit seat to be doctors. But with all that I am grateful to the tuberculosis patients - after all, they are responsible for my food, shelter, clothing and education.

The newer medicines came later. They changed the entire outcome and the outlook of the disease. The victory over Tuberculosis which at one time seemed to be imminent now looks distant and even impossible. We are already feeling the "power" of drug resistance. With the emergence of MDR (Multi Drug Resistance) and XDR (Extended Drug Resistance) and TDR(Total Drug Resistance) looming large, we will be probably returning to the bygone era of "no drugs" worth mentioning for the dreaded killer disease! Tuberculosis!

THE STORY OF SANTOSH - A CHEERFUL PATIENT

In the beginning of the 2 nd year training during MBBS, the students get to see the live patients for the first time. The students have to talk to the patients, examine them meticulously, see the reports, present the case to the teachers and discuss with them. The patient's problems will be discussed with and by the senior doctors and explained to the students. The whole teaching process is called «bedside clinics» and is a much awaited event by the students.

The attire worn for attending the bedside clinics includes an apron, a stethoscope, and clean and fresh garments. A special feature is that all students seniors and juniors participate together in this without any discrimination. However, the case presentation is usually done by the senior students who are about to appear for the examination. The junior students observe the seniors and help them in the history taking and get prepared slowly for such experience in future. The whole duration of such activity lasts for about 1 t 2 months at a time. This is known as a "clinical posting".

In this duration students get to see many cases. The best part is interaction with the patients. We went to our first clinical posting with a lot of hesitation and inhibition and expectations. We were afraid of the teachers. We knew our limitations. But we were eager to learn. When we went to the ward on the first day, the first patient we observed was a short boy of about 18 years who was stunted and looked about 12 years old. He was a cherubic kid with a round face and prominent chest. He always had a ready smile and would cooperate with us freely for the clinical examination. All of us were fond of him and he was fond of us too. He would go out of the way to put the new young students at ease. We asked him the details of his illness as a part of history taking. He gave a fantastic story which was very impressive. He said he is suffering from "asthma".

Santosh was having spells of cough, breathlessness and wheeze since early childhood. His illness drained his family's meager savings and he was not getting any better. He went from one doctor to the other. And then he went in for herbal medicines - some roots were advised to be brought from far off forests. He would tell amazing stories of how his "uncles" went to far off land s to get them. We would be awed by the stories and charmed by his mannerisms. Later the doctor whom he consulted asked for the tiger's milk. Uncle first had to find a lactating tiger and then get its milk - heroic indeed! Finally when nothing seems to cure him permanently, he came to the Government Wenlock Hospital where he could consult any good doctor free. In fact he was in the hospital for over a year. When he was well, he would help other patients and also the nurses to distribute food and medicines. In all he would keep us entertained and informed.

One day we found him in a bad shape. He was very ill. He was blue and cyanosed. Confused and comatose. His body was swollen due to water logging. He was in Cor Pulmonale with Respiratory failure. This was not typical of asthma. Then we asked Post graduate students. We did reading from textbooks and research. We realised that the boy was not suffering from asthma (an eminently reversible condition) but from Cystic Fibrosis rare genetic condition which can involve multiple organs - Lungs (Emphysema, Lung abscess, pneumonia, respiratory failure); Intestine (constipation, failure to pass meconium, malabsorption); Endocrine organs(Diabetes); Altered sweat content and other things. They can eventually go into advanced emphysema (he indeed had a huge chest) and respiratory failure the hallmark of which is Cyanosis (bluish hue). Hypoxia (lack of oxygen) can also produce bluish discoloration, confusion, headache among other features. Then suddenly I realised something - the disease was not asthma; it was a much more serious, irreversible disease inherited genetically (autosomal recessive pattern) and the exciting stories s never happened - they were all born out of the Hypoxic state with low oxygen I could not just believe that there were no willing and daring uncles; no tiger's milk; no herbs and roots brought from far away lands! The boy who was always cheerful and always willing to help and cheer up others was very ill and comatose. However, he seemed very peaceful. We stood around his bed feeling helpless. We held his hands, thanked him and assured that we will pray for him and indeed he would be fine by the next day. We had a sense of sadness because he had become a part of our family. Next morning when we went to the hospital to Santosh' bed it was empty!

USING DIGITAL TECHNOLOGY AS A USEFUL TOOL IN MAKING CLINICAL MEDICINE MORE AFFORDABLE

There was a time everything was inexpensive and the expectations of the patient were very limited. Patients used to profusely thank my father if they improved a little bit. In fact, some were so good in that art that they got away without paying anything! Both the doctors then commanded highest respect and the patients simply adored them.

Slowly the technology evolved. With that the "costing" came. Machines were a double edged weapon - they made the diagnosis more precise for the patient and the process of treatment more remunerative for the doctor - still, the things were not expensive! Doctors still commanded respect and admiration.

Then came the modern digital technological revolution - doctors found it time saving - they could take some short cuts and get away with it - after all, the technology always helped them! This came at an exorbitant cost - naturally the patients expected perfection in diagnosis and treatment and always a cure! The doctors started to get sued because of overlooked diagnosis (what could be easily identified with a good clinical examination can be missed with the best of machines) - giving a drug to which the patient is seriously allergic to without asking him is case in point.

What then is the solution? Should we shun the new technology? No, I never said that! Is there a way out? Surely there is. First step is to spend time, take a good history and do a thorough clinical examination. Then comes the surprising part - I refer you to a video gone viral on the internet where the idea is mooted by a foremost invasive cardiologist Dr. Eric Topol - He uses a smart phone (an I phone) which has a specially made card - the card can be used for 2 tests ECG and ECHO cardiogram by just applying it on the chest of the patient - takes much less time and will cost a fraction of the cost to the patient - an usual ECHO costs $800 and done using this technology this costs much less(around $ 100). Considering that there are 2 million ECHO s done per year in the USA alone, you can imagine the savings. Dr. Topal has also incorporated some more things - calorific value of foods - You ask the smart phone how many calories are there in a given meal or a combo promptly the answer comes. It also tracks the blood sugar values depending on a wireless sensor implanted in the abdominal wall. While a patient requiring a continuous monitoring goes home, a wrist bound monitor with the digital screen will help track all the required parameters at home. The best part is all this data can be collected wirelessly and forwarded to any computer. All this tracks the patient continuously at a fraction of the cost.

What is good for Dr. Topol ia also good for us. We habitually ape the west. This is one thing worth aping. We can use the same technology or modify it to suit our needs. Incidentally, Dr. Topol has written a book "How digital revolution will create better hospital care". Such of you who have the time and want to know more can please read it. The link for the original video is here https://www.youtube.com/watch?feature=player_embedded&v=r13uYs7jglg

I am sure the message is clear - use the digital technology as our slave and not be a slave of the digital technology. This will help evaluation of the patient, diagnosis, management, life style modification and domiciliary treatment even in the presence of fairly severe illness. It gives us a golden opportunity to do the best and get a firm grip over the patient care again! Long live "Digital technology controlled by man!"

A MYSTERIOUS CASE OF THE "UNCONSCIOUS PATIENT" - A TRUE HUMAN INTEREST STORY

I was really impressed by the old man when I saw him in my clinic. A crisp, spotless white dress; clear thoughts; good ability to communicate stood out. He was always in control. He came with his wife looking less than half his age - a very young wife indeed. He made it very clear that he had come for one time consultation for a thorough check up and advice.

He had no specific complaints. The check up after a thorough clinical examination showed that he had aged gracefully and had no major illness, in fact not even diabetes! Only thing I was not clear was his occupation - he simply said that he was a "trade union leader" at Bombay and had made some enemies in the course of his career.

After about a month, his wife requested for a house visit at their flat for what looked like a bad bout of respiratory infection. I obliged considering his age. He recovered promptly. On my way out of the building, I met an old friend of mine who also was residing in the same building. He was shocked I had visited his house. "Be careful", he said, "this man was a "supari" hit man at his prime at Bombay"! I was indeed surprised and slowly forgot all about it. He had mentioned that his children were studying in a residential school far away and I now seemed to understand why - In his old age he had become a toothless tiger and (he along with his family) was therefore vulnerable to attacks from his enemies.

About a year later, his wife phoned at the dead of the night. She said that he was very ill and requested me to come immediately. It was raining cats and dogs and I was not very eager to go. I tried telling her to take him to a hospital. My wife then reprimanded me saying how can a lady alone get her husband to the hospital without help. I went ahead to his house.

Imagine the scenario - Dead of the night and it was raining very heavily. The old man had fallen unconscious at the entrance of the bathroom - his head and part of the trunk inside the bathroom and remaining part of the trunk and the legs outside. He was unconscious and breathing heavily. He did not respond to his name or to the painful stimulus. I knelt down in the dampness and checked him - BP was normal and he did not have any stroke. The question that bugged me was why indeed was he unconscious?

The first step in any treatment is a good diagnosis. There was none here. I had to be very careful now. Just then the wife said "Now that you have seen him you may go. Tomorrow I will come for the death certificate". I was shocked. I told her I had not completed my job. She coolly told me she did not expect me to! I was in a dilemma. whether to leave him alone or to diagnose and treat him. I had to think fast. I looked around and checked what I had hitherto ignored - the drugs. To my dismay, I found a strip of a strong anti diabetic tablet with 3 tablets missing. He was not a diabetic. The diagnosis was obvious - he had been given 3 tablets of a strong anti diabetic medication causing a low blood sugar (hypoglycemia) enough reason for explaining his unconsciousness!

I decided to save him as it was an eminently reversible condition - ran out of the flat, woke up the next door neighbour who happened to my same old friend whom I had met earlier, shifted him to the hospital with his help. You should have seen his wife's face. If looks could kill, I would be dead on the spot. He recovered fully and went home.

I slowly sorted out the remaining part of the mystery. His wife wanted him dead to claim his wealth and property. The hit man almost tasted a generous dose of his own medicine

EXAMINATIONS THAT WE FACED - A NECESSARY EVIL?

One of my favorite medicine teacher used to describe examinations in general as "a botheration to the population of the Indian nation whose main occupation is cultivation". Examinations during MBBS are no better. Most of us still get nightmares about appearing for the examination. The general pass percentage those days was 30% which meant 2 out of 3 students who appeared failed; only 1 passed! One therefore, we appeared for the examination expecting a failure! Those who cleared all subjects in the first attempt without failure naturally were the best and could clear any examination national or international they chose to appear later.

This brings back some memories of examinations we faced during the MBBS course. We had theory and practical exams. Theory exams consisted of 5 questions of 16 marks each (essay questions) where long answers were expected.

The 6th question was for 20 marks which was subdivided into 3 or 4 short note questions. For those who had prepared well there was not enough time to complete the paper. Those who had read little, there was nothing to do for 3 hours - either way this was complicated! If one answered all questions, he barely managed to pass - it was always possible to find out what one missed! There were a few students who would habitually appear for the exam every 6 months and fail. They were "super casuals". During the exam, I was surprised to find one such person writing continuously for 3 hours. He failed! When I asked him for the reason, he said "didn't match"! I asked him "what didn't match?" He said he randomly wrote 6 answers(he had prepared only that much) without reading the question paper hoping these answers would match the questions- and unfortunately it did not match with the question paper! Then, there was this guy who brought ready made answers to expected questions in various parts of his body - folded chits hidden in collar, folds of shirt, below the belt, inside the socks etc. Why did he fail then? He lost the master index slip telling him where he had hidden each piece and so could not locate any paper!

Clinical exams were a different ball game - students have to examine patients and diagnose them. Better students go by the clinical findings. The others go by the incidental clues - Red lungiwala has Mitral Stenosis. On one occasion, the patient had a bath and changed his lungi before the exam with disastrous consequences! Worse still, a patient visitor came wearing a red lungi and he was told by a 'super casual' that he surely had Mitral Stenosis. When the person strongly objected the student persisted the official list says so "But you are wearing a red lungi!" The tuberculosis patient had no slippers - so said the list - the day before the exam a philanthropic organisation donated slippers to some poor patients. The patient of tuberculosis was not diagnosed properly because of that! Another clue was the bed number. The patient on bed no 7 was supposed to be having anemia due to malnutrition. To the bad luck of students the patient went home the previous night and the new patient was fat and well fed. Despite the obvious, the student presented this case as thin and undernourished much to the dismay of the examiners!

As a part of the examination some specimens were kept. One part of the liver was kept in a jar of formalin. The professor asked the student "What do you think would have happened to the owner of this liver?" meaning thereby what disease he might have suffered from-was the student in a position to tell by looking at the given specimen? The student coolly replied "I should be able to answer your question after a few days". Perplexed, the examiner asked him why so, for which the student replied "I expect him to be alive as he has he remaining part with him. He therefore will surely come looking for this part too!"

The cake was taken by a clinical exam in Surgery. A student was appearing for the 6th time. The examiner took pity and and decided to pass him on one condition - he cannot practice Surgery and that he has to promise the same keeping his hand on Bhagavat gita. The student did so and he passed. Everyone including the examiner was surprised to find him join MS Surgery the next year. The examiner asked him why did he not keep up his promise. The student replied "I will do my MS sir - that is for getting a fat dowry. With that money, I will build a good hospital. I will never operate. In fact, I was wondering whether you could join after your retirement"!

GROWING UP WITH CRICKET

It was a Sunday - a bright and sunny Sunday. India was playing a test match against Australia. We had a group of friends who were in love with cricket. We wanted to" watch" the match. There was no TV those days. We however had a willing neighbor who had a huge Murphy radio. All of us would sit around the Murphy radio. There would be about 15 of us of different age groups. The oldest one sat with a A4 size paper and a pen. We would listen to the radio commentary - usually by the likes of Vijaya Merchant. He would describe the scene so well and one could visualize the whole thing as if it was happening right in front of one's eyes. That was the clarity of language and communication!

Mr. Vijaya Merchant would start "This is Vijaya Merchant from Brabourne stadium Bombay; the sky is clear, the batsman is ready, the bowler is looking around at the field placements; 3 slips, 1 gully, 1 mid on, 1 mid off ......" We would draw the field on the A4 paper, mark out the fielder positions, and track the ball as it was being bowled and played. Another boy would be the "score marker". We would indulge in this for 3 hours before lunch and then reassemble after having food in our respective homes. This was a very satisfying experience. Doubts would be cleared by the older boys. Every one got a rich experience of almost "being there". However, this was possible only on Sundays and holidays.

On all days we would assemble in a compound of a government school whose compound wall had fallen down. At the evenings we would play cricket from 5 PM to 7 PM on all days including the days of examination. There boys of various ages would meet and play together. The youngest (between 6 to 9 years) would be only allowed to stand in the periphery and watch. After maybe 1 year, they would be allowed to pick balls crossing the boundary line and then throw it back to the bowler. Boys who were a little older would be allowed to field. Later, batting and bowling would be permitted. The best ones played competition matches. The others stood watching and cheered hoping to play sometime in future. There was no scope for misbehaviour and cheating. The punishment for cheating would be to get thrown out of the peer group which none wanted and therefore everyone obeyed.

Looking back, these things helped us a lot in shaping our personality. We had seniors to look up to and ask for help. 3 of the boys got selected at various IITs for education. Some became engineers. A couple of the boys became doctors. Some became bankers and one boy in particular did exceedingly well and went on to become a director in the bank in which he worked. One person became the correspondent of the Sri Ramakrishna Vidyashala at Mysore and later went on to become the President of the Mysore Ashram which he still is. Many years ago, he did a ground breaking research on cloning of plants from the leaves in a small, ordinary laboratory Sri Ramakrishna Vidyashala at Mysore. He would have figured on BBC had he been in UK.

We were unified by the game of Cricket which we grew up with. We had role models among our own friends and peers. They led by example. We had working models of leadership, camaraderie, sharing, give and take, respecting seniors, accepting verdicts and decisions which may not have favored us, losing a game, and above all, fairplay and truthfulness. I remember one episode when a boy threw a stone at another boy who had lied. The boy got hurt in the head by the stone and bled a little. When the parents asked him how it happened, the boy simply said "hit by a lie!" He recovered uneventfully and such a thing never happened again.

THE STORY OF THE APRON (WHITE COAT) - HOW MUCH WE ADORED IT!

Our entry into the clinical side after clearing a major ordeal of passing I MBBS (Anatomy, Physiology + Biochemistry) was publicised by two eagerly awaited events - wearing of an apron (white coat / lab coat) and the stethoscope for the first time. Those things gave some recognition to the clinical students and brought the students closer to being «real» doctors. I remember even the public giving importance to these. It was highly fashionable to wear them to a movie! Even the students who rarely attended classes, invariably wore them while going to a movie theater or a restaurant. There was one particular photo studio which had an apron and a stethoscope and anyone could get themselves photographed wearing an apron and putting the stethoscope around the neck! One of my relatives who was not educated beyond the high school had his own photo taken in this fashion and that photo occupied the place of pride in his house! A third year medical student going on a Yezdi motorbike with his girlfriend wearing a stethoscope around his neck and an apron (mostly borrowed) was indeed a sight to watch!

The real use of a white coat was in the biochemistry lab - How can we forget the yellow stain which developed when Nitric Acid fell on it? Trousers or shirt would have been ruined but for it. Pockets allowed us to keep our instruments and papers. Sometimes small holes developed in the white coat due to sharp objects. One could "diagnose" where the student is posted by the prevailing smell of the apron. A strong smell of formalin meant that he was doing Anatomy, a horrible smell of gangrene meant he was in the Surgical posting. A clean apron was much in demand thing during the exams!

Now, a little bit of the history of the white coat. The first time the white coat was allowed by the law to be worn was in 1699 in France.- it was then referred to as a "long robe". The Columbia University medical school founded in 1767 was the first one in the USA to award the Doctor of Medicine degree (MD). It was also the first medical school to have the "White coat ceremony".

What happened to the white coat? Many professions other than the doctors started using it to gain respectability - laboratory workers, people in the food industry, barbers to name a few. What is the perception of the current generation about the white coat? What does the research show?

For one thing, the doctors still feel it is important and they like it and prefer to wear it to work. The patient's perception has however changed. The patients feel that the apron does not invoke the same satisfaction or confidence as it did earlier. They would be as comfortable with a doctor who does not wear it. So a white coat does not form a part of the formal attire any more!

Is it safe to wear white coat? We are not talking about the safety for the doctor here but about the safety for the patients. Now come the surprising findings of research - Risk of infection is probably INCREASED by the white coat! They are talking about the BBE scenario - which means Bare Below Elbow.- no wrist watches, no rings, no bracelets, no bands. A strict "Wrist hygiene" has to be practiced to avoid bacterial contamination from cuffs, sleeves of the apron / shirt. A strict Hand hygiene is required during the insertion and care of invasive devices - urinary catheters, intravascular shunts. White coat contamination by the bacteria (staphylococci of various types) is now widely known. The remedial measure of removing and hanging up the white coat before entering the patient's immediate environment is suggested and practiced.

How often a white coat has to be washed? How best is cleaned? The best way is probably to launder it. Best method is to send it to the hospital laundry. However, if one decides to launder it at home, using a hot water wash cycle with a bleach is probably the best option. Along with the white coat, the other things to be suggested to be regularly decontaminated include cell phones, ID Card, purse, bags and jewelry.

What does the future hold for the white coat? Does any one care?

THE STORY OF THE STETHOSCOPE - "HALLMARK OF THE MEDICAL PROFESSION?"

The stethoscope is one thing which each medical student waited eagerly to possess. A hallmark of the profession it was the passport to the clinical years. Pre clinical years were dull and drab. It was very difficult to learn a subject like Anatomy but very easy to fail. With great difficulty when one almost lost faith in oneself and all interest in the subject and all hope of passing, one would pass and got into the clinical side. This desperate individual got to possess the stethoscope - the transformation was almost unbelievable and magical. The same student would be looked upon as a "senior" by the students then in the pre clinical years and would be the cynosure of their eyes! The stethoscope also brought the student closer to being a "real doctor".

What is the story behind such an important invention? It can be said that this invention was born out of child's play! Rene Theophile Hyacinthe Laennec saw 2 children transmitting scratching sounds through a roll of folded paper to each other. This was the first stethoscope! It avoided the direct contact of the ears to the body (which had to be done till then). When he reported his invention in a journal, it was immediately taken up and translated widely. This invention (in 1819) made Laennec immortal. He became more famous than Auenbrugger who had become famous for his invention of percussion as a modality of clinical examination. Sadly, later Laennec succumbed to Tuberculosis.

Laennec not only invented the stethoscope but also named the lung sounds so heard (sibilant and sonorous rales); and was the originator of the terms like aegophony and whispering pectoriloquey. It was also found to help in the auscultation of the heart. Naturally it became popular with the practicing doctors and medical and nursing students.

I clearly remember possessing a basic model of the stethoscope. It cost Rs. 30 at that time. Better models like Littmann were expensive, lot more than Rs 1000 and were beyond the reach of common students. They were also the target of theft. I also remember the commotion caused by the theft of a Littmann stethoscope of one of the students from Malaysia. Everyone's bag was checked; it was never found. Once my ordinary stethoscope was stolen. I was wondering what to do. The next day, it promptly came back to the place where I had left it! Indeed, the thief had a class and he showed it! It was customary for the professors to demonstrate the main findings to the students - this included the auscultatory findings also. On one occasion, a senior professor, known for his sarcastic humour, reprimanded a student saying that the student's father should not be stingy and should buy him a better stethoscope so that he can hear the findings better. Everyone started giggling hesitantly for the student was none other than the professor's own son!

No wonder this instrument held the sway for almost 200 years. It seemed to be irreplacable to generations of medical students and doctors. Doppler ultrasound and ECHO gave it a big blow. An Echocardiogram was more reliable in some situations. The postgraduate thesis done by one of my PG students proved this. There were some situations where the stethoscope still proved superior. It has been observed that the Cardiologists are using the stethoscope less and less.

Now HHUS (Hand Held Ultrasound) is giving the stethoscope a serious competition. Though expensive (about $10000 a piece), it may be more objective and more accurate. There is no evidence that the stethoscope improved the patient outcomes in its early years though it helped in better diagnosis of Congestive cardiac failure and some other potentially dangerous situations. The lives were saved only after the better drugs like diuretics became available. HHUS on the other hand can do much more. With the basic training, even the non doctor peripheral workers can pick up dangerous conditions like Cardiac failure and Pulmonary Embolism and save lives. Rural health workers can be made to diagnose abnormal fetal positions and fetal distress early and inform the doctors thus helping save lives. With mass production and encouraged sharing, the working cost may also come down.

Will we see the sad demise of a legendary icon of the medical profession shortly? Only time will tell. Let us wait and watch.

MYSTERIOUS CASE OF THE "MEDICAL MURDER"?

Some patients are persistent. He was one such. He was a bank manager who had intestinal tuberculosis 5 years before he contacted me(in 1988) and was treated at AIIMS for the same. The diagnosis then was confirmed at AIIMS using a barium meal which was then a standard procedure for evaluating esophagus, stomach and small intestine. He had all records with him running into well over 100 pages and later he was successfully cured. 5 years later, some of the symptoms like abdominal pain returned and he consulted me for the same. The clinical examination was completely normal and the picture did not suggest intestinal tuberculosis. So I tried to convince him that we shall get an abdominal ultrasound instead and think of the barium meal. He was not willing. He insisted on a barium meal saying that it was that investigation that had picked up the right diagnosis at AIIMS. I wrote out some blood tests and a barium meat and forgot about it.

A week later, I had a strange phone call from the radiology centre telling me that a patient of mine had developed intense abdominal pain after a barium meal and was very uncomfortable. They wanted to know whether I wanted to see him or he could go home instead as somebody else from his town was willing to take him. I insisted on my examining him and on examination found that he was very ill and having abdominal tenderness and rebound tenderness suggesting peritonitis. A peritonitis due to leakage of barium is a serious matter as 9 out of 10 patients are likely to die despite an attempt to treat them well. The puzzle was if he had indeed developed a leakage of the barium from the intestines, how did this happen as the intestinal wall is quite thick.

I admitted him and involved a surgeon to help the patient. The surgeon was the best I saw in my career but due to some health issues, his career was seriously cut short. He also was equally curious and took the bold step of exploring the abdomen to know the truth. On exploration, a sizeable amount of barium was found in the peritoneal cavity. The surgeon did the detective job and found a small hole in the intestines from where the barium had leaked. On a careful scrutiny he found that there was a small abnormal looking spot on the liver. He was intelligent enough to take biopsy from both the sites (intestines and the liver). He went an extra mile in that he stayed 3 nights in the hospital in the patient's bedside to take care. The relatives were highly appreciative. They understood the predicament and the cremation was over in a few hours.

The next week, I had an unexpected visitor - a "cousin" of the patient from Bombay. He told me just 2 things. One that I was responsible for the death of the patient which he called a "Medical Murder" - he was referring to the fact that we had got a barium meal without indication when abdominal ultrasound was available! The other thing he told me was that he had called a press conference the next day so that he can appraise the press and the public of this human interest story and successfully ruin my career. It was then the seriousness of the whole thing struck me. I was speechless! I had to think and act fast. I tried telling him that I had ordered a barium meal at his request and that depended on the fact that the intestinal tuberculosis was picked up at AIIMS with that investigation. He flatly denied that the patient was treated for any disease earlier. He had destroyed the records!

I understood what he wanted. He wanted money. He spelt out the amount. I could not even think of paying it - I felt there was no fault on my side. Nor could I afford to pay it. But I had to have some concrete proof. I did the best possible thing under the circumstances - I asked for time and he gave me 1 day!

I went home, sat alone and thought about the whole thing. Was I responsible for the "medical murder" directly or indirectly? If not, how could I get out of the mess? Suddenly I realised that there was indeed a way out - to get the histopathology reports of biopsies from the 2 sites - intestines and the liver. I personally went to the place to have a look at the slides. What I saw was something unbelievable - Intestinal malignancy with secondaries in the liver!

It did many things - It gave us the truth; It explained the hole in the intestines (the cause of the peritonitis), It saved my practice and reputation. I did not have to worry about the threats. I could fully justify my actions ethically.

The remaining story is indeed short. The "cousin" could not believe his bad luck and I could not believe my good luck! When he came the next day as he had said he would, I congratulated him for solving the "Mystery of the Medical Murder"!

MYSTERY OF THE "HIDDEN ENEMY"!

She was a brilliant student. Her father, a banker, was worried about her cough and evening fevers. She ate less, would tire easily and had lost weight. A careful history, examination, a chest x ray and blood and sputum examination confirmed it as Tuberculosis of the lung. She took the treatment, followed the advice and recovered fully. In the bargain her father became my good friend. He mentioned another daughter of his who had settled in Maharashtra after her marriage.

After about 2 years, he came back with the other daughter. She was almost looking like her younger sister. She was feeling tired nowadays and had come to her parental home for a few days. She wanted a check up. Nothing particularly was complained of. On a thorough examination, I discovered mild fever and a lymph node mass with a few enlarged lymph glands sitting on the right Carotid artery in the neck. It felt like a tubercular lymph node mass (with features of matting). Ideally a Fine Needle Aspiration or a biopsy was required to prove the suspicion. The location being tricky and the finding classical, I deferred this step in the interest of the patient a decision I regretted later. However, I explained the whole thing to her father and made him feel the gland mass so that he understood my dilemma of avoiding the procedure of Fine needle aspiration/ biopsy to avoid a possible damage to the major artery which was a more serious matter. I started her on standard doses of anti tubercular medications and monitored her temperature and weight on alternate days.

She was to go back to Maharashtra in about 2 weeks and she was much better by then. Fever had settled and she had gained about 2 Kg weight (as expected). Her father was very satisfied. She returned to her home without any issues and started leading a normal life.

After about 5 days, she started having fever. They phoned me. I asked her to rule out Malaria which was rampant in Mangalore at that time. There was no evidence of Malaria. I asked her to contact a local doctor. What followed was unbelievable and gave me a rude shock. The local doctor on examination was able to feel lymph gland mass on the left side also and wanted a biopsy of that. It was far away from the Carotid artery and therefore it was very safe to do so and it was done. The nightmare followed. The report came as Papillary Carcinoma of the thyroid gland - a variety of thyroid cancer. The doctor even went to the extent of telling her father that the original diagnosis was indeed wrong and cancer was missed and was treated as tuberculosis, an unpardonable mistake. He phoned me and politely told me so.

Now it was my turn to get seriously upset. I had entirely depended on my "fingers" for the diagnosis - my chief always told me after 10 years of my training I was ready for the "bare hand combat" and should always trust myself. I had indeed believed him and trusted myself. I could have done at least an ultrasound scan or a CT scan of the neck and the mediastinum and picked up the "hidden enemy". Did I entirely miss the track? How could I make amends?

I suddenly realised that the whole thing depended on the biopsy done on the left side. Why not do a biopsy on the right side? Why not a CT scan to know the extent of the disease? Indeed, why not? I requested the father of the patient that they must get a CT scan of the chest and mediastinum and do a lymph gland mass biopsy on the right side also. It took me a while to convince them I also asked them to consult the senior most physician in town and lay all the cards on the table. Let him give a verdict.

The CT scan showed involvement of multiple groups of lymph glands in the neck, chest and the mediastinum. The biopsy from the neck glands on the right side revealed the presence of Tuberculosis! I was right! What was the message? There were 2 different diseases on two sides - Tuberculosis on the right side and cancer on the left side! A rare and a deadly combination indeed! The other take home message was to avoid a short cut whatever the reason is. A scan would have revealed the other glands and prevented all embarrassment.

There is a little more to be added. The senior physician who saw the patient and the reports thoroughly appreciated my approach for being patient friendly and using good brands of the drugs, following up the patient systematically without admission and keeping the patients informed of everything at all times. He even advised the father of the patient to thank me. He promptly did so and we became friends again!

A hidden enemy indeed!

TRUE STORY OF TYPHOID MARY - DID SHE DESERVE TO BE MADE A VILLAIN?

Typhoid fever was a dreaded disease. It could spread easily through food and water, make the victim very ill, and could even kill them in large numbers before a treatment was discovered for it. This story of Typhoid Mary dates back to the early 1900 s 1906 - 7 to be precise.

How would you feel if you are shadowed, followed. chased and arrested when you feel you have done nothing wrong? That is exactly what happened to Mary Mallon, who later became famous as Typhoid Mary.

In the summer of 1906, Charles Henry Warren, a banker, took his family on a vacation to Oyster Bay where he rented a cottage from one George Thompson. All was well till August 27. Then one by one starting with one of Warren's daughters followed by 2 maids, then the gardener, and then the other daughter - all became very ill due to typhoid fever. Thompson was worried that no one might rent their cottage and so wanted to investigate this in detail. He knew typhoid spread through food and water but could not guess how so many could get the disease at the same time. He therefore hired George Soper, a civil engineer, to find out the truth. Soper believed that the cook was responsible in some way as the disease spread mainly through food and water. It so happened that Mary Mallon was the cook and he took note of that fact. Now the problem was to prove it and the main stumbling block was that she was completely healthy and the concept of a "healthy carrier" was not yet known.

So, Soper did the next best thing - he traced the employment history in detail back to 1900. He found that typhoid outbreaks had followed wherever she had worked. He found that, in all, 22 had developed typhoid fever and 1 young girl had died from 1900 to 1907. A good detective work indeed - this is called an epidemiological survey - a sort of fact finding. He felt it was more than coincidence. He wanted to meet her where she was presently working as a cook - the house of Walter Brown. She did not like the idea one bit - she chased him away with a kitchen knife. Not an easy one to get rid of, he came back with a helper (Dr. Bert Raymond Hoobler). Both were successfully chased away by an enraged Mary. He then involved the health department and Dr. S. Josephine Baker was sent to investigate. This time she saw a team approaching from the health department and staged a "vanishing act" - she was nowhere to be seen and later was traced to the hidden compartment at the basement of the neighbor's property which she accessed after running away jumping over a fence and entering through the secret trapdoor. She was forcibly taken to Wilard Parker Hospital in New York. She was investigated and was found to harbor typhoid bacilli in her stool. She was later forcibly transferred to an isolated cottage at the North Brother island near New York.

She seriously believed that she was wronged. She questioned the wisdom and purpose of arresting and isolating her - a healthy lady who according to her had done nothing wrong in her life. She failed to understand why she was being hounded, chased and arrested and kept in isolation.

The government promptly quoted 2 sections to justify their act - sections 1169 and section 1170. which said that the board of health shall use all reasonable means for ascertaining the cause of disease or peril to health, and for averting the same throughout the city. It was also considered that the fact that she was healthy made her more dangerous as a source of such a serious disease which no one would suspect her to be the source of. Hence her imprisonment and isolation were justified. She fought a lone battle saying there was no proof that it was she who had spread the disease. In 1909, the case against the state was taken up by a judge who did not agree with her. It was argued that even people infested with the typhoid bacillus could pass the disease from their infected stool onto food via unwashed hands. Cooks and food handlers were the people most likely to spread the disease in this fashion. Mary Mallon, by now famous as the "Typhoid Mary" was sent back to confinement.

In 1910, she was allowed to go free as long as she agreed never to work as a cook again. She hurriedly accepted these terms to regain her freedom, gave an assurance by affidavit that she would never work as a cook again and would take stringent measures to prevent any further spread of typhoid by regular washing of hands. "Typhoid Mary" walked free.

What do you think? Was she indeed a villain as made out by her sad story?

GOING TO SCHOOL - SOME CHILDHOOD MEMORIES

I studied mostly in the Kannada medium. I hardly remember what I learnt at the schools but vividly remember some of my teachers and my friends. But I very clearly remember the schools and the process of going to school every day.

In fact, we looked forward to the activity of going to school everyday. We walked to the school. We would go along with our friends. There were many trees on the way. They belonged to no one in particular. There was a mango tree. We would throw stones at the tender mangoes and sometimes succeed in getting a couple of them. We always shared what we had. We did not have anything to cut with. We did the next best thing - strike the fruit to the floor and share the pieces! That some one got a bigger or a smaller piece did not matter - what mattered was we all got a piece each!

Then there was a tamarind tree - boys loved the mature tamarind - We would pick the fruits from the roadside and share and eat them. I cannot forget the sweetish - sour taste of the tamarind from that tree. Friendships were built on sharing the tamarind fruits from other sources. I remember explaining mathematical problems to my friends and getting sweet tamarind in return!

There was a ice candy vendor just outside the school. None of us had any pocket money - so we could not think of buying one! When we were thirsty playing in the school, we freely drank the municipal water. And we played every day during the last period. There was a great camaraderie and all enjoyed the games. That we played was all that mattered we did not even bother to see who won.

We had to have only 3 vaccinations - small pox, BCG and Tetanus toxoid out of which the first 2 were given in the school. That we picked fruits from the 'dirty' floor, drank 'unclean' water and had fewer immunizations made our immune systems stronger and we got allergy and asthma less often. Now there is a lot of emphasis on 'very clean' food and water and too many vaccines are given and deworming is done too many times and too often in the pediatric age group resulting in an imbalance between the T2 and T1 immune lymphocytes causing allergy and asthma. There is a move in the west to encourage children to eat from the table tops so that they are somehow exposed to some infection. so that the rising incidence of asthma is reversed.

In the rainy season, a holiday would be declared if many children got wet. There were no autos and it did not matter when a holiday was declared. On a very rainy day we would intentionally fold our umbrellas and stand outside the school building for 2 to 3 minutes. We would get soaking wet and the headmaster would take pity on us and send us home. We of course had a different agenda. There were paper boats to make and to be left in streams of water which flowed vigorously during the rains. It gave us immense pleasure to watch our tiny paper boats travel fast in the steam.

Then there was the much awaited craft period twice a week. We learnt to make kites and magic lanterns. The craft examination consisted of making a kite - the success was gauged by one's ability to fly the same. Almost every boy succeeded in succeeded in flying his own kite!

The day began with a prayer We were taught prayer songs from different religions. Significance of each day was explained. Each festival was celebrated. Diwali was celebrated in a unique way - each one would get some crackers and give them to the class teacher. They would be collected and equally shared among all. Sharing equally was the rule - no one objected.

Then there were yearly picnics - usually to the nearby places in and around Mangalore. The parents of some children gave food, some gave beverages - mostly home made - Some helped by accompanying the children so as to help the teachers in controlling them

You thought I forgot to mention homework and exam! Not really! There was no home work! Non at all! All studies were completed at the school. There was no need for tuition. Teachers in the schools gladly cleared the doubts. Revision classes were held just before the exams. Exams were a routine affair - we were scared of the examination but were well prepared for it.

If you ask me did I love my schools, my answer would be "Yes, of course"! But i would shudder at the thought of having to go to school today as a student simply because such schools simply do not exist anymore!

THE STORY OF" QUEEN OF BLUE HEARTS"!

The year - 1930; the hospital - Johns Hopkins; the department - Paediatric; the doctor - Helen Taussig, a specialist paediatric cardiologist rightly considered by some as the «Queen of hearts».

Her dedicated team was puzzled by the short lived, strikingly blue skinned babies which they called the "crossword puzzles". She could decipher a part of the puzzle - the death was due to lack of oxygen - as revealed by careful autopsies. Obviously, something in the heart was hindering the process of oxygenation - the mixing of deoxygenated and the oxygenated blood at the level of the ventricles was probably the reason. The valve of the pulmonary artery through which the blood from the heart reached the lungs (where it got oxygenated and purified) was narrowed.

Taussig now looked for the possible solution. When no obvious solution was found in the living children, she started to look at the answer for the misery of blue babies in the fetal circulatory system. Ductus arteriosus was a special path to bypass the unnecessary trip of the blood to the lungs (as the lungs never oxygenate the blood in the fetus). But once the baby began breathing, the lungs start oxygenating and ductus and other similar paths normally closed.

Taussig noticed that the blue color intensified when the ductus began to close. She made a clever observation - the children still needed the ductus(for their survival.) but for a reverse purpose. The normal process of the closure of ductus sealed off the path of the blood to the lungs and virtually killed the baby preventing any oxygenation / purification of the blood. If kept open in the blue babies after birth, the ductus gave one more chance for the deoxygenated blood to get purified. She was thrilled to have found a way to keep them alive longer!

Now she had to find a surgeon who would agree with her ideas, believe her and do the surgery boldly. No one had thought of this or done this surgery before! Taussig had heard of a doctor who had daringly entered the heart of a young girl to seal off an improperly closed ductus. If he could seal off one, she reasoned, he could be convinced to create one. She went to Boston in 1940 to meet him. In her own words, she was devastated to find that "he was not in the least interested" in the possibility of building a ductus

Then it so happened that a nationally known and acclaimed vascular surgeon Alfred Blalock joined Johns Hopkins hospital. She was in awe of him when she witnessed him close a ductus successfully. She said to him "but the really great day will come when you build me a ductus for a child who is dying because too little blood is going to the lungs".

Accepting here challenge, Blalock started experimenting on dogs. After doing so on hundreds of dogs, finally he was ready for the first patient in early 1944.

The concept involved in the surgery was simple - to choose a major artery stemming from the aortic arch and join it to the pulmonary artery. This procedure sent some of the blood back to the lungs. The result was spectacular and was there for every one to see!

"I walked to the head end of the table ', Taussig recalled of an operation on a young boy "and there he was with bright pink cheeks and very red lips"! Blalock - Taussig shunt was born and many children got a new lease of life.

All this was possible due to the careful observation and logical deduction by a compassionate doctor - Helen Taussig - "Queen of hearts" indeed!

EVIDENCE BASED LABORATORY MEDICINE (EBLM) - ARE WE TAKING THE "EVIDENCE" TOO FAR?

There was a time, not long ago, when the clinician diagnosed the condition the patient was suffering from entirely based on a detailed history, a thorough clinical examination and a few simple tests. The verdict was accepted without any questions. The possible expected course the disease would take and the expected outcome were discussed. Most of the time, the predictions came true. What was being practiced was "Experience based medicine". It was accepted and had stood the test of time. However when things went wrong, some disappointment was inevitable. Most of the time the turbulence settled down. Litigations were few and far between.

Somewhere in the 1990 s the experience based medicine gave way to evidence based medicine. Every disease entity was defined. There was a need to fulfill 'required' criteria to conclusively diagnose and start treating the same. Evidence therefore was needed to diagnose conclusively after ruling out other possible differential diagnoses; to know the stage, severity and extent of the disease and document the same; to prognosticate the outcome and if possible to help improve it. Diabetes mellitus is a case in point - hyperglycemia is a good pointer but exact sugar value gives a rough idea about the current severity. It is every doctor's observation that the patient either eats less or doubles the dose of the medicine on the day of check up to get a better blood sugar value to impress the doctor. Estimation of the glycosylated hemoglobin alerts the doctor as it is an average of 3 months' blood sugar values and cannot be 'doctored' by one day's efforts! Ketone bodies if present in blood and urine alert the doctor as the diabetic ketoacidosis is a serious life threatening complication.

Acute abdominal pain is another scenario - when the surgeon has ruled out all important surgical causes including gall stone colic, appendicitis, ureteric colic and when the physician has ruled out all important medical causes like diabetic ketoacidosis, acute pancreatitis, peritonitis, usually one has to think of acute intermittent porphyria a condition which can only be diagnosed by a simple urine test for porphobilinogen - a striking example where the evidence based laboratory medicine becomes indispensable. Even to diagnose acute peritonitis, one has to get values of serum amylase, serum lipase, serum calcium and other data. These also help in assessing the severity and prognosis (Ranson's criteria).

Imagine a scenario where a young athlete hits her head against a hard surface and loses consciousness. There are no focal neurologic deficits. The CT scans are normal. A clinical diagnosis of "concussion" is made. What is the evidence? Till recently, there were none. Now they are trying to correlate the values of T- tau protein levels in CSF taken at serial intervals - immediately after the event, 12 hours later, 36 hours later. The first peak immediately seen after the concussion settles in 12 hours. The second peak comes between 12 and 36 hours. 1 hour values help to decide the time likely to be taken for the resolution of concussion and the time taken by the players to return to the game safely. Hence T - tau is an important' biomarker 'of concussion.

Then comes the most common and the most important scenario - acute chest pain. Acute myocardial infarction is the most important event to be excluded. There was a time ECG was enough. Then came the enzyme biomarkers. Enzyme CPK came just when I started to practice. It was a sensational discovery! It would not only help pick up the diagnosis but also would help us quantitate the extent of myocardial necrosis. I remember a particular patient referred by a psychiatrist saying "The ECG is normal. His CPK values are 2500. Where is the heart attack?" Truly, there was no heart attack - the extreme elevation was from the skeletal muscles - the patient had Myxedema (hypothyroidism). Soon Isoenzymes came and CPK MB was considered the most sensitive marker of a heart attack. Then came the Troponins - C, T and I of which T and I would help diagnose cardiac muscle necrosis. The problem however was that the elevation was seen even when the cardiac muscle got damaged due to non ischemic conditions as remote as a scorpion bite. Something more specific was obviously needed. Very recently, highly sensitive cardiac troponin T (hs cTnT) has become available and is now very helpful. The sad news though is that CPK MB has gone out of use and died a natural demise - most f the labs are not doing it any more - thereby showing that there is a 'shelf life' for these biomarkers!

I am sure, we have to understand that the EBLM (Evidence Based Laboratory Medicine) has come to stay. We cannot wish it away. The physicians have to extend an olive branch to the biochemists, use the EBLM and make the best use of the available options. It will help themselves and the patients.

Long live EBLM!

A STRANGE CASE OF PATIENT DIAGNOSING HER OWN "MYSTERIOUS" ILLNESS! - TRUE MOTIVATING STORY OF KIM GOODSELL

$\mathbf{M}$any a time patients want to know more about their own illness. Giving them information could be a tricky process. Mistakes happen - in the form of too little / too much information being given. Finally both the doctor and the patient give up.

I remember making patient education information files about common diseases. It helped me immensely in saving my skin in one particular episode where the patient refused angioplasty and the next day died. His immediate relatives who were abroad were very upset. Only when I showed them what was discussed with the patient and showed them the documented evidence that he had refused the options, they cooled down.

Most refuse to be told micro details and possible complications. Even when the patients are seriously ill, after listening to all that is told to them, they ask the same question "no problem, isn't it?" "No other problem, but we are having enough of them to go by" I tell them.

Then comes a patient once in a way, who is like a breath of fresh air - the one who asks pertinent questions, understands the answers, and discusses intelligently - a pleasure to deal with. Like all good things, these patients are rare to come by. This is the story of one such exceptional patient

Kim Goodsell in San Diego at the age of 30 started noticing 'a strange instability'. That was 20 years ago when she was training for an ironman triathlon. She was diagnosed with 2 rare diseases. One was a disease giving rise to palpitations - ARVC (Arrhythmogenic Right Ventricular Cardiomyopathy) which is known to cause fatal arrhythmias. She got a cardiac defibrillator implanted (as required) and started getting excruciating pains. She could not even hold a fork!The second rare diagnosis came in the form of a neuropathy which caused progressive degeneration of the muscles for which she had to undergo hip replacement due to a dysplasia of the hip. The disease was CMT (Charcot - Marie - Tooth disease) type 2. She gave up the rigorous training and In 2010, asked the physicians at the Mayo Clinic whether her 2 ailments were related. She was told that the odds for having the 2 diseases together were less than 4 per million that is even lesser than the chance of one being hit by an asteroid! She next consulted the geneticist who tried to dissuade her by saying that it would cost her $3000. But she wanted clear answers. She had found out that she had the the LMNA gene the mutations of which can cause bone disease, cardiac disease, neuropathy, systemic degradation. She insisted, spent for herself, got the test done and then came the surprise - the test was positive

This was the beginning - she started to study the molecular pathways of the products of the LMNA gene - She found convergence of lamin A/C and desmosomal proteins. The mutations on the LMNA gene were pertubating the downstream desmosomal proteins. She not only studied the problem in great detail, she wrote a dissertation on it and even set up her own treatment plan! She started on a diet that she followed strictly no excitotoxins (glutamates); no gluten, solanin contained in pepper, tomato, eggplant which she had loved to eat before.

Her outlook on life changed Her health improved, relations with other family members improved and she could walk without support. She could even travel and participate in the outdoor adventure with her husband. She felt she had reversed the disease process.

Her physician, Dr. Topol, feels that she is a great inspiration for other patients and even the physicians. Physicians are indeed shocked to know that she had deciphered the mystery of her own rare diseases and taken steps on her own which helped her not only to get better but also to reverse the disease process! Of course, the advanced technology stood by her and helped her. This was impossible 5 years ago.

What differentiates this patient - Kim Goodsell from others - she had an 'insight' a single minded focus and energy to understand her disease; a gut feeling (born out of research and knowledge) to go ahead with the expensive gene tests despite being dissuaded. She stood to gain a whole lot! She did not waste time on self pity and performance of useless rituals!

We only wish there will be many more Kim Goodsells! Then the interaction with the patients becomes more interesting, more meaningful and rewarding to both the patient and he doctor!

AN AMAZING TRUE STORY OF A NEAR PERFECT MURDER - "THE ACID BATH MURDER CASE"

Before I narrate this story, I must set the stage. In 1973, I was studying Forensic Medicine. It was one of the subjects I liked best. A great fan of detective and crime fiction, I was enthralled by the various stories pertaining to crime. There was a very good reason for it - Professor Laxman Pai - a very well read person with a fluent Shakespearean English and a fantastic skill of narration was our professor of Forensic Medicine. He would narrate the stories pertaining to crime, detection and poisonings which would hold us spell bound. No body would utter a word. Everyone attended his classes. We adored him and his stories. The story I am going to tell is one such which I shall never forget!

Around 1940 s, the victim, a well to do Kensington widow was lured to Crawley, shot, stripped of a fur coat and jewelry. An attempt was made to get rid of her body.

The law at that time said that if no body was found however strong the circumstantial evidence was, no one could be convicted. The murderer wanted to take shelter behind this rule and walk away scot free. And he almost did. How did he get caught? That is the most interesting part of the story!

Mr. Haigh, who allegedly murdered the lady, immersed her in a tub of commercial sulfuric acid for some days and then when almost everything got dissolved, he buried the few remains in the surface soil in a yard rented by him. Almost everything was dissolved in the strong commercial sulfuric acid - well, almost everything. The dentures, the gall stones and fragments of a few skeletal bones were not dissolved mainly because the Haigh had impatiently taken out the body a bit too soon out of the "acid bath". The dentures were conclusively identified by a dentist as being made by him for the missing woman. This evidence was not contested. Haigh confessed to 5 other similar murders which he had got away with. He was found to be guilty and hanged.

It was a near perfect crime. It is one of my favourite stories - the "Acid Bath Murder Case". I have narrated it to many batches of students. This story was invariably followed by a question to the students from me. "What is the poison you would use if you wanted to execute a perfect murder - the poison should have no color, no odour, work fast and be not easily traceable". May did not answer. many were not confident. I used to ask them to look up. Most never did. One particular student once said he could not find the answer in any book - what next. I jokingly said "Ask Professor Laxman Pai". I could not imagine what followed. He went to Professor Laxman Pai and asked him the question - "How to kill someone with an unidentifiable poison and leave no trace?" Now a flabbergasted Dr. Laxman Pai asked him "Who wants to know?" Without batting an eyelid the student said - "Dr. Raghavendra Bhat. "Now it was Dr. Laxman Pai's turn to get surprised - he took the phone (landline in those days) and asked me in a very surprised voice "Raghavendra Bhat, what are you up to?"

Needless to say I have stopped asking that question after this episode. But the story of "Acid Bath Murder Case" does not stop amusing me -for it was a very cleverly and near perfectly executed near perfect murder case- almost perfect did I say? A little impatience on the part of the perpetrator of crime sent him to the gallows- a near perfect murder indeed!

THE TRUE STORY OF SIR RONALD ROSS - "MOSQUITO MAN" - HE GOT EVERYTHING ONE DREAMT OF! - WAS HE HAPPY?

Many would have heard his name - Sir Ronald Ross - in connection with the dreaded disease Malaria. He did a lot of research and proved that the disease was transmitted by the mosquitoes. He even got a Nobel prize. He was knighted. He was made the member of the Royal society of Medicine. He should have been the happiest person on the face of the earth. Was he? This is his true story giving details of his life and an insight into his personality.

He was born in India on 13 May 1857. He loved poetry and music. He passed his exam for the Royal College Of Surgeons of England in 1874. His father's dream was to see him enter IMS in India at Madras which he reluctantly fulfilled. He was not too happy with the way his career was progressing. He took a year's leave (from 1888 - 1889) and completed his Diploma in Public Health from the Royal college of England. He became interested in Malaria in 1892. Initially he even doubted the existence of the malarial parasite! He took a long leave in 1894 and met Patrik Manson in 1894 at London. Manson convinced him that the malarial parasite did indeed exist by showing him the Leveran bodies in blood (which were really malarial parasites in the patient's blood demonstrated by Leveran in 1898) and also showed him that these can be seen better by staining them. This was to be the turning point in the career of Ronald Ross.

Convinced by the belief that mosquitoes were in some way connected with the disease (Malaria) a concept proposed by Leveran and seconded by Manson, Ross agreed to do further research in India as requested by Manson. For the 3 years of the study, Manson would be the voice for Ross. He worked at Secunderabad while he got an answer for his problem.

Now, study this scenario - Ross was given a room at Secunderabad hospital. It was a small hot room with only a window, a fan, a table, a chair and a microscope. His job included catching 7 mosquitoes everyday without harming them and carefully dissecting them ti study their gut - to see if anyone of them had malarial parasites inside their gut. Not even one mosquito studies was not yielding the result that he wanted. To make the matters worse, he could not even open the window or put the fan on. The dead mosquitoes awaiting the dissection will get scattered. The sweat from his brow would fall continuously on the microscope thereby ruining the fine adjustment. Imagine the constraints he had - he somehow managed to work. Later when he almost quit, Manson prevailed on him to continue for a few more months. On the 25 August 1897, Ross had last 2 mosquitoes left to be dissected. and then it happened - Ross found some large, clear cells in the gut of the mosquito the malarial parasite thereby proving his speculation that the Mosquitoes transmitted the disease. This was reported in the BMJ 0n 18 Dec 1897.

Worldwide recognition, name and fame soon followed. He was awarded the Nobel prize in 1902, Knighthood in 1911. He was also made the member of the Royal society of Medicine. Despite all these Ross was unhappy. Mentally he started competing with his mentor Manson whom he now considered an equal. He had many achievements more than Manson but Ross's private practice simply could not match the private practice of Manson who was immensely more popular with the patients.

This probably started his downfall. He contacted Malaria. He got severe depression. In 1927, he had a stroke from which he partially recovered. He died on 16 September 1932 a sad man.

In all, it can be said that the days of his research in India were his' golden days'. The non collaboration and disagreement between Ross and Manson after 1900 seems to have temporarily halted the development and progress of British Tropical Medicine.

What is surely of interest to the readers of these blogs is the fact that he served at our own Government Wenlock Hospital at Mangalore during his tenure at IMS. We should be really proud to have studied from and worked in a hospital where a Nobel Laureate had once worked!

A VISIT TO THE DOCTOR'S CLINIC (AN OFFICE CONSULTATION) PAST, PRESENT, AND FUTURE

I have very fond memories of patients visiting my father's clinic for an outpatient consultation in late 60 s and 70 s. The atmosphere was one of happiness and joy. There was a high degree of respect given to the doctor. The consultation began with the exchange of pleasantries. An enquiry about a close family member son / grandson / father / grandfather was the opening sentence. This was followed by the usual questions and a clinical examination. A chest X Ray, and a few basic blood tests were done if really required. Urine sugar helped to pick up diabetes which was then investigated in a laboratory. The consultation ended with a sound advice and a reassurance. The patient was invariably accompanied by many family members wife, sister, mother in law, children and others. This was a sort of a day out for them. Most were coming from out station places like Kasargod, Hassan, Coorg and this was an outing. The consultation was followed by a lunch at a restaurant, and then a movie followed again by some shopping. Then they went home usually by the last train / bus. No wonder therefore the patients liked the visit to the doctor's office and looked forward to it. Obviously an "experience based socially laced medicine" was being practiced much to the satisfaction of the patients. I remember one particular patient of mine, a lady, whom I saw at an institution that I was working at that time. Her son would bring her every month by train for a chronic backache. I would see her and she would go away by noon. On one particular day, I found her waiting for me in the evening - I was really surprised to see her waiting. On asking her why she had waited, she simply said "Doctor, you did not pat me on the back and reassure me as you always do!" I then realized the importance of this one simple gesture!

Then came the changes. There were more investigations available. The whole process became customised and standardised. Less time was being spent with the patients. Slowly the emphasis was shifting from "reassurance" to "cautious observation" and a specific and accurate diagnosis. This probably reduced the satisfaction and trust in the doctors. Consumer courts started and slowly "defensive medicine" started taking over from "experience based medicine". The doctors did not see the writing on the wall.

I remember an interesting episode which happened to a senior surgeon of Mangalore. On account of an MS Surgery examination, the doctor who was an examiner for the examination, reached his clinic only by 6 PM though he was to reach by 12 noon. A patient who considered himself important was visibly agitated and gave a vent to his feelings.

He rudely said to the doctor "Where were you doctor? I waited for you for 6 hours!" The doctor was naturally a witty one. He coolly said "I waited for you for 30 years. Where were You?" The patient was speechless!

In 1990 s, the "evidence based medicine" started taking over. The wit, humor, wisdom, social interaction and trust were slowly replaced by arrogance, cut and dry approach, mistrust, a feeling that the things were being done for a "gain" by the doctor. The distance between the doctor and the patient increased. Doctor shopping began. This was the time when Corporate entities made an entry into the hitherto sacred and private space of doctor patient interaction. Health was converted into a "product" and the doctor, a "service giver"- just like any other service for gain! Naturally the respect of the patients vanished and doctors were merely performers and service providers for a fee! This trend increased the patient expectations tremendously and a good result was always expected. The costs naturally went up and the satisfaction levels plummeted. We are currently experiencing this.

What will be the future of the patient's office visit? A survey by doctors at the US showed that the patients did not like to wait for 1 hour for a 7 minute long consultation. Dr. Eric Topol feels that the Smartphones will have an important role to play in the whole process in future - Eye examination, ENT examination, transmission of metrics like BP, Heart rhythm, respiratory rate, oxygen saturation can be conveniently and easily done using a smart phone without the patient's presence in the doctor's office. Dr. Topol even expects the hospital visits to happen in a completely different way in 5 years from now. Video links with transmission of data in real time or in advance - a form of virtual office visit may replace most of the conventional office visits.

Do not ask me whether the payment for the virtual consultation will be real or virtual an image of a high denomination currency sent with a thank you note to the doctor but the patient using WhatsApp! I really cannot tell!

TRUE STORY - HOW THE GREAT NEUROLOGIST BABINSKI WAS DENIED PROFESSORSHIP - DID IT REALLY MATTER?

It is not possible to achieve all the ambitions all the time. Can one still reach great professional heights and have a good career? an average man's answer would be a 'no'. But I warn you not to draw conclusions before reading the outstanding story of Joseph Babinski, undoubtedly a great neurologist of all time.

Babinski was born in 1857. He was a faculty of Medicine in France where the faculty was given only part time jobs and allowed to practice. A university career was possible only after defense of thesis. Aggregation (becoming an associate Professor) was the next step. This entailed complicated exams. The next would be elevation to the post of the Full Professor (which was partly by selection) and gave a status and enabled one to head the department.

The time had come after Babinski became eligible for appearing for a competitive examination after completing 2 years of residency. These exams started in 1802 when the success rate was 60%. Babinski appeared in 1877. He did fairly well in Clinicals (anatomy of trapezius 17 /20) and treatment (Burns 20 /20). He did not qualify for aggregation and was promoted to permanent post in 1879.

After completing 4 years of residency, Babinski appeared for the Gold medal examination which was mandatory. He did well in the written examination (Gastric mucus membrane). He qualified for the oral exam but could not appear due to the illness. He was not considered for the gold medal.

He got employed under Charcot a well respected neurologist at that time. In 1886 he appeared again for the Aggregate exam. He scored 16 / 20 (Hydatid cyst) which was not good enough to appear for the orals. In 1887 he appeared again with Gilles de la Tourette and Pierre Marie, scored 16 / 20 for clinicals and 14 / 20 for orals (chicken pox) and was not admitted. In 1888, in a competition held for 3 possible places Babinski scored 27 / 30 and in orals (sclerosis of the heart) he got 26 / 30 - not good enough for the next step.

In 1893, he competed for the aggregate and he successfully completed the exam with a score of 30 / 30 for written part (Scarlet fever) and 19 / 20 for orals (diphtheria with paralysis)., 17 / 20 for cliniclas, and 30 /30 for the case (Syphilis). The idea was to find an able successor to the then head of the chair - Charcot. The competition was between, Babinski, Landouzy, Dejerrine, Raymond and P. Marie. Babinski was the preferred pupil. Unfortunately, the arch rival of Charcot - Bouchard- was at the chair of the selection committee. Babinski was intentionally ignored. This story was lapped up by the press and the media much to the discomfort of the education minister who was involved by the public in the controversy. Next opportunity was provided in 1895. Babinski never appeared. He vowed never to appear again. He joined a hospital at la Petie where he worked for rest of his illustrious career.

Did Babinski lose anything by being unfairly denied of the opportunity? In his own words, "No" is the answer. His only regret was that he could have influenced the career if he had any. He in fact considered it an advantage not having been invited. He could work at his own pace in his own style.

What is the moral of the story? One does not necessarily have to be a professor to excel in the field of practice of Medicine.

Dear friends, do not get de motivated if you do not achieve what you want to. Still you can do well. In fact, Babinski became world famous for his sign even without Professorship.

"DAMSEL IN DISTRESS" - A TRUE EPISODE - WHAT WAS THE REASON? HOW WAS IT SORTED OUT?

Whenever a lady comes for the complaint of vomiting, I remember this episode of a «Damsel in Distress». It was a usual day like any other day. She had taken an evening appointment. She was working in a software firm and wanted an urgent appointment to consult me.

She came with her mother. Mother was really concerned to the point of being inquisitive. The complaint was one of vomiting almost after each feed. Mother and daughter lived in different cities. Daughter had come to her mother's house because of the complaint.

After taking an elaborate history, mother hovered around the daughter during the examination. At every step she would ask "What is the diagnosis?" The daughter was uncharacteristically quiet. She spoke little but co operated for the examination. Those were the days before the ultrasound scan became available. At the end of the examination, I asked for some blood and urine tests. In situations such as these one discretely asks for the pregnancy test - I used to use a code "Urine for H" (which my regular lab understood) indicating HCG which is the basis of the pregnancy test.

She came back with the reports. She came in alone and said "I insist you do not divulge anything to my mother. I also insist you help me in solving the problem. I know my rights and I demand professional secrecy even from my mother. Then she went out and called her mother in. The report confirmed my suspicion. She was indeed pregnant! Mother asked me "What is the diagnosis doctor?" I had to think fast. I had to tell her something that would closely mimic the early pregnancy. Something that had vomiting as a component. I said "Urinary Infection". Indeed, ascending infection can be complicated by acute pyelonephritis which can present with vomiting (and fever which can get masked by the partial treatment). Mother seemed to be satisfied with the explanation. Daughter kept quiet. Both of them went back.

Next day the daughter came alone. She demanded, "Now that I am your client, you are duty bound to help me. Guide me to a good doctor for the termination of pregnancy". I suggested some name and she went away. She came back after a couple of days and thanked me. She gave a vent to her feelings. She said a man gets away easily and a woman has to suffer and all this is very unfair. I agreed with her. I almost forgot the episode.

After about 5 years, I saw her again in my clinic accompanied by a man. She had come to consult me for something very minor. Anyway, I did my job professionally and did not show any signs of recognition. She thanked me, went out with her husband. Just after she left I observed her handbag. As I was pondering what to do and how to get her back, she suddenly came in. "Doctor, I am sure you recognize me. Doctor, do you remember I gave a vent to my feelings and had said the boys get away. After going back to work, I gave it a serious thought. I wanted to punish the guy who did it to me. I married him. What better punishment can I give? I wanted you to know that the whole episode had a happy ending.

I was speechless! I congratulated her and wished her well. How many girls can do this? More should try to "punish" the person responsible. I could not decide who was in a greater distress. The "damsel" or the "gentleman"?

THE STORY HOW AND WHY THOMAS WILLIS (OF CIRCLE OF WILLIS FAME) BECAME VERY FAMOUS

Thomas Willis was a British doctor who was known for neurology and anatomy of the brain- best known for Circle of Willis

He was born in 1621. His research would change the concepts which prevailed before his era. In the pre Willis era, the teachings of da Vinci, Vesalius and Berangario prevailed and brain was thought to be an organ of purification. Willis did a lot of work on Anatomy of the brain. He worked in collaboration with Christopher Wren and Richard Lower. His research in anatomy of the brain resulted in findings which were unexpected and very different from the views held then. He became famous. But for his research he needed to dissect human corpses. It was not easy to get them and many a time those were obtained by a 'forcible' donation

Today's story relates to one such episode where the body for research was obtained by a 'forced' donation - one Anne Green, a 22 year old housemaid who became pregnant by the grandson of her employer. She gave birth to a baby prematurely and hid the infant which promptly died. She was accused of infanticide, tried and convicted and was to be hanged to death for the offense.(This happened on the 14th December 1650) This was a public ritual witnessed by many. They pinched her and pulled her down by the legs which was supposed to shorten the process and thereby reduce the duration of agonising asphyxia. Her body was pulled by so many people so violently that the court official was worried whether the rope would break and requested the people to leave the body alone. The body was given to William Petty for anatomy lectures at Oxford. When Petty and other doctors including Willis opened the coffin, the 'corpse' was said to have taken a breath. Willis raised the body to a sitting position the doctors opened the mouth and poured hot drinks down. This caused a cough and the doctors began to resuscitate her by rubbing the hands and feet. About 15 minutes later the eyes fluttered. The doctors began bloodletting and applied compression bandages to the arms and legs to increase the circulation (as it was believed then). They put her body on a bed besides that of another woman whose unfortunate job was to keep Anne's body warm. 12 hours after the official 'execution' Anne spoke a few words. After 4 days, she began to eat solid food. After a month, she was said to have fully recovered. Because of her unique resuscitation, Anne was later reprieved of her crime. Anne moved to the countryside taking the coffin as a souvenir. She married, had 3 children and lived for another 15 years.

Willis married Mary in 1657 and in 9 years of their married life had 8 children 4 sons and 4 daughters. All but 2 children died. Mary expired in 1666.

This episode made Willis very famous and his success resulted in jealousy from his colleagues. He had to face a lot of harassment He died relatively young at the age of 54. Willis is best known for his circle of Willis which was described before him and he always acknowledged the earlier claims.

It is rare to find such an extraordinary story in the history of Medicine - No wonder it made Willis world famous for all times to come!

MYSTERY OF THE MEDICAL FITNESS FOR A PARALYSED PERSON OR WAS IT IMPERSONATION?

In the career of a doctor there are some sticky situations. Insurance Medical examination is one of them. This is mainly because the scant respect the administrators and the agents have for the client, medical report or the doctor. I really do not understand the logistics of this. The payment for the doctor is still about Rs. 100 - while foreign insurance companies pay $ 250 per report! Cheap labor indeed. Again I do not understand this mentality particularly when the emoluments of the staff are increased almost on yearly basis for their work(?).

This story concerns one such medical examination a mandatory requirement before any insurance. A person was brought to me for a LIC Medical examination. I did not know the person though he is supposed to have been a well known person. He was accompanied by the ABM (Asst.

Branch Manager) and the LIC agent. I requested both of them to identify the person and sign on my LIC diary for the same. I sincerely examined him. I found him feverish and surprisingly a little bit pale which was unusual as he was coming from a good family. I even commented about it and he promptly said he was suffering from cold.

The ABM and the agent took possession of the medical certificate, thanked me and left. I forgot about the episode till about 2 months later the agent told me in passing that the client died and that the claim (double benefit 4 lakhs for policy worth 2 lakhs) was promptly rejected by the LIC. I was not concerned anyway. Later I came to know that the party had filed a suit against the LIC. I did not bother about the details. Only when a person from the Udupi division of the LIC walked in a few days later for the "inquiry". Even then I did not assess the severity of the situation. I thought it was a routine inquiry because of early death which is a standard procedure. I was shell shocked when the person said the LIC had decided to file a criminal case against me. Why so?

He gave his version. The man was in a hospital admitted for a widespread cancer with spread to the bone, fracture of the spine and paralysis due to compression of the spinal cord. It was highly impossible that he could have come out of the room in the hospital leave alone visiting my clinic on the first floor. I got the implication. I had examined an impersonator. LIC wanted to file a criminal case against me for 'criminal involvement with the client for gain'. I was speechless. They gave me a week to reply.

I visited my lawyer friend in the evening and explained the situation to him. He heard me out and coolly said,

"These things happen. Say sorry. Usually they leave you!" I was really upset. I had not committed the fraud. LIC officials had. To save them they were trying to make me the scapegoat. I sat up the night and gave it a serious thought at midnight when all is quiet and one can think without distraction.

I hit upon an idea which seemed to be foolproof. I wrote back saying "The person alleged to be so and so who was examined by me on the said date was indeed medically fit. However, the onus of identifying them lies with the persons who introduced him - in this instance - the ABM and the agent of LIC. So please forward your queries and inquiries to these two who in my opinion are hand in glove with the party and are the perpetrators to the crime".

The tone, and the content of the letter must have annoyed them. The LIC decided to take a second opinion from Nani Palkiwala. They wanted to silence me. I proactively wrote to them that I would be unilaterally proceeding for defamation charges with a claim of 1 crore for the mental harassment from LIC in order to save the fraudsters who were from LIC. The letter had the desired effect. Nani Palkiwala advised LIC to lay off and behave. They apologised. The case was closed.

The moral of the story is to be very careful at all times. Fraudsters plan the escape route in advance. Innocent one gets involved unless one is vigilant at all times!

ON BEING A MEDICAL TEACHER - MY EARLY EXPERIENCES AND EXPERIMENTS

Being a good medical teacher was my life's ambition I had seen a few dedicated teachers during my MBBS days. I recognised the efforts they put in ; the sacrifice they made and the devotion with which they imparted the knowledge. I did not have to look far. I had zeroed in on my career.

The day I passed my MD, I applied for the job - Lecturer in Medicine. I was greatly disappointed to know that there were no immediate vacancies. I joined a hospital and patiently waited for the vacancy to arise. While working there, I developed interest in collecting clinical materials-case details, X rays, ECG's etc which were very helpful later as teaching aids and for the books I wrote. I also developed a habit of referring to the books and journals.

The golden day came on 17 February 1982 when I joined a medical college as a Lecturer. I went with a new apron;

new shirt, and armed with knowledge, capped with pride and arrogance (born out of knowledge). Initial years of one's career are 'power driven' - you 'know' everything. From the knowledge stems arrogance and from that comes a dynamic performance. There are only 2 zones - black and white.

I was ready for my first clinics.

What followed was unimaginable - the senior students had already attended a clinic by my chief (Dr. KP Ganesan) and left. 4 students were curiously looking at me. They said they were repeaters. There were no organised classes for repeaters. They wondered whether I could teach them. I had taught such students as an intern and as a PG student. I agreed immediately. I took the class well. They liked it. I was extremely happy. I still remember the names of 2 students - Bipin Patel who later become a Physician in the US and did very well for himself. The other one was one Sandra. For the next 2 months I took clinics for them regularly and all 4 passed (the pass percentage then was 30%). I was thrilled.

I have taught many batches of UG s and PG s after that. I enjoy using the black board for the theory classes. There has been innovation and modernization in teaching. Power point presentations have replaced blackboards. I personally feel that the audiovisual aids like power points impart uniformity. They extend mediocracy. Basically it is an exercise in transferring image(and not necessarily knowledge) from the teacher to the taught without either one essentially understanding or mastering the topic. A black board is like an empty canvas. It gives immense scope for the teacher to evolve the subject and develop the concept. It is an exercise in transfer of knowledge with a better understanding by both - the teacher and the student.

The salary of a teacher was unimaginable when I joined. I took home a princely salary of Rs. 250. Daily wage unskilled laborers earned more. Then it was a matter of pride to be a teacher. To survive one had to practice. That is how and why I practiced. Even now my first and only love is teaching. Practice is incidental requirement which I never really fell in love with except the fact that I met people and I enjoyed interacting with them.

One or two things have concerned me. Till recently there was no formal training for teachers who teach at highest level -MBBS, MD, DM, Phd. etc. Also no emphasis is given to the 2 major requirements in any field - communication and decision making. Innate skills of communication have to be honed. Decision should be made on rational thinking and common sense rather than using guidelines and protocols alone.

The later part of one's career is passion driven. One is aware that there is a grey zone (in addition to the black and white) and many things belong there. One humbly accepts the fact that one could be wrong or more importantly, the other person could be right. Arrogance born out of knowledge (of the early phase of the profession) is replaced by humility born out wisdom in the later phase of the profession.

Probably I am now in the 'passion driven' phase of the profession. I travel far and wide on invitation to take classes and teach PG s and doctors at many CME s.

I want to emphasize one important point. A good professional remains a student and a teacher all his life.

One need not necessarily have an attachment to a medical college to be a teacher. Teaching any one else at the work including junior doctors, colleagues, even the patients (patient education) makes one a teacher. What is important is to perform the task well and not worry about the title.

Looking back, I have no regrets. However, the satisfaction obtained by teaching the repeaters and the so called back benchers (who really need us and our skills) was infinitely more than that obtained the day I received my 'good teacher award'.

MEMORIES OF MY FIRST MBBS EXAMINATION - SWEET DREAMS OR NIGHTMARE?

One of my Professors used to say "Examination is a botheration to the population of the Indian nation whose main occupation is cultivation." I would like to make a correction - they are so for all nations irrespective of the occupation!

The most horrible examination I faced was the first sessional exam after 6 months after joining the I MBBS. It was important to be in the top 40 of the class. It meant an entry into the Anatomy Club which almost ensured a pass in the final exam. I felt this should be a cakewalk, for I was the 13 th in the state in PUC to qualify for an almost free merit seat. The books were bigger, the subjects vaster, but the overconfidence brushed it aside. I worked just as I had worked for PUC. I never realised that was not enough. When the results came, I was in for a rude shock. I had scored just 37! Faced with defeat, humiliation I accepted the result and went to the teachers for advice. One of them encouraged me. He said "You can still try. If you score 105 together in the first and the second sessionals, you will get a direct entry to the Anatomy Club and you will become a Prosector which means you can teach the juniors the dissection (you will get one more chance for some dissections) and also get paid for it. It was a win - win situation and I tried really hard. I learnt to draw really good diagrams copying from my friend's uncle's diagrams. I did really well and got 69 out of 100 - just crossing the magic figure of 105 by 1 (a total of 106). I understood what hard work was.

The final examinations were considered to be necessary evil. All appeared, only about 30% passed. Going to the exam hall was like going to the slaughterhouse. No one could predict the outcome. When the son of the Principal of Mangalore college appeared for Physiology at Manipal, where the Dean was the examiner he promptly failed. Neither the Principal (his father) influenced nor the Dean thought of passing him on terms other than on merit.

That reminds me of my own Physiology exam. "Effect of Atropine on the Vagus nerve and the Heart" was the task It needed to dissect the tiny Vagus nerve and study the effect of Atropine and get a cardiac muscle curve as the proof. It was an examiner's delight and the student's nightmare. With my limited knowledge of finding the Vagus nerve (a white, smooth, glistening hairlike structure), hampered by my astigmatism, I could never locate it. After the stipulated 60 minutes one had to face the" firing squad" I mean the examiners! I realized at the end of 55 minutes that I had only 1 option. To kill the poor frog! I had to commit the crime in 5 minutes and that too without leaving a trace. I had to think fast. The only weapon I had was the Atropine. I emptied the bottle of atropine on the heart of the frog. After a series of twitches, the frog promptly died and the curve became flat. I washed up the scene of crime and no trace of atropine was left. The army of examiners came to me. I was so scared. I was sure I would fail. They asked for the graph. I said "The frog died!" The senior most among them said" I have seen these kind of things happen. I fail to understand how the frog died at the correct moment? How on earth did you kill it? I put up a brave front and said "Sir, it must have had a heart attack!" I answered all the questions. I just passed. Anything was better than failing!

Anatomy was another issue altogether. Dissections were the toughest party of the examination. Each got 1 part of the body to dissect - selected by lots. The stipulated time was 3 hours. The one who got to dissect the sole of the foot usually went home straight away - that was better than failing after a 3 hour struggle. Luckily I did not get that!

Histology though a difficult subject to master, was the easiest exam. There was one George, who trained the students in a unique style. He was very good at drawing and anyone who attended his classes would learn to draw well. He would tell us how to recognise each slide without error. Cover slip broken on the right side - Heart; Cover slip broken on the left side - Lung; Excess stain on the back of the slide - Testes; Slide broken in the right corner - Prostate..... the list would go on. He would show us these peculiarities repeatedly. He had only one request - "Please do not break a slide!" With this 'foolproof" training, almost everyone passed!

Lastly there was Biochemistry - a part of Physiology. It would boil down to 2 questions in Physiology out of which 1 would be a cycle. There would be a 'titration' experiment in the practical examination. One had to carefully neutralise something (usually an alkali to an acid). End point was important. The professor always said "add half a drop more"! I never understood how to add half a drop. The smallest is one drop! Once when I asked this doubt the professor said "Only a vigilant student can do it well". May be I was not vigilant enough. I never understood the half drop concept anyway.

I did pass the first MBBS exam in the first attempt! I even scored well! Looking back, that looks incredible!

THE LARGER PICTURE - DO NOT HOUND THE DOCTOR WITH A "TELESCOPIC MENTALITY" - DOCTORS SHOULD PROTEST!

Road traffic accidents are common. The injured persons are brought to the hospital (government or private). Doctors attend. Results are unpredictable. If the results are good, the people feel «Doctors did their duty. So what?" If the results are bad, the people get agitated. They feel that the doctors did not even do their duty. Usually this is followed by manhandling of doctors and destroying the property of the hospital. Doctor is neither protected nor respected. A weak case is filed against the perpetrators of crime and the sympathies of the public lie with them. The harassed doctor and the hospital get no accolades, thanks or good comments.

You may say "Why a blog on this common scenario?" I will explain. This, I must remind you is an incomplete picture. A telescopic view of a larger picture. What then is the larger picture? A person buys a bus (Bus owner) without any worry about its quality. A driver employed by him drives it as if he owns the bus and the road. An unscrupulous employee at the RTO certifies it fit even without checking it. Road is made by the unscrupulous elements in connivance with the city administration. In the case of a RTA who then is the main culprit? Your guess is as good as mine. I can say for sure one thing - not in the least the doctor. Why then harass him? Because he is the "soft target in the unorganised sector". What then is the solution? Seeing the larger picture and involving the real culprits. If there is a need for expensive treatment and / or expensive investigations naturally the bus owner and the city administration must chip in. Do not they blame the hospital owner if there is a death? Similarly bus owner must be arrested and taken to task. Why does this not happen? I really do not know

In case of a food poisoning, the hotel owner, cook, building owner, food inspector, and the city administration must be tackled and if at all the doctor must be praised and applauded when helpful. Why should the brunt of the burden borne by the doctor?

Also, I would like to make a clear distinction between the 'error of judgement' and 'criminal negligence'. Not attending is criminal negligence. There is no excuse. Attending but making a wrong diagnosis amounts to an error of judgement. This is. pardonable

How shall we tackle these issues? Creating awareness is one thing. Forming a SOP is another. If the item you buy is defective, the onus is on the manufacturer and not the salesman. You cannot shoot a messenger however bad the message is. Doctors have to assert their rights.

Creating awareness involves many platforms. Honoring of good doctors, appreciating the good deeds, recording the contributions in disaster management are all important steps. Doctors should proactively take credit by using internet, facebook and other similar sites. Petitioning on the Facebook is another option.

The whole idea is to get credit for the good acts and expose the real culprit. Service clubs and Professional organisations like IMA must also help. It will take some time for things to change. A change from the telescopic view to viewing the larger picture is the need of the hour. I hope that it will happen pretty soon!

EXPERIENCES INSIDE THE LIFT - DOES IT REFLECT OUR CIVIC SENSE OR WE ARE ALWAYS IN A HURRY?

In the olden days, one always climbed the staircase. The expectations were simple - to reach the destination. Climbing the stairs was a pleasurable activity. We could chat with the others and exchange views. I remember my chief telling me how he had suffered an attack at of angina pectoris at the age of 35 and then became fit enough to climb staircase. He would never allow us to use the lift (later days)even while climbing the 6th floor. Sometimes we would have a cup of coffee after climbing down the stairs. Thus Intellectual and social interaction formed a valuable part of the stair climbing exercise.

Then came the era of lifts (elevators) and later escalators. Climbing became effortless and fast. People forgot the use of staircase. I still prefer staircase. In emergencies, I use the lift. When I climb down the staircase, I find really ill, disabled, patients with COPD and breathless individuals slowly climbing up the staircase. When I ask them why they are not using the lift, the answer is the same - they just could not get into the lift - they were kept out by the fitter people! So much for the social understanding and compassion from the society!

When there is a designated "doctor's lift", it is common to see the public beat the doctors to it. I once had to explain a group of people that I was the person they had come to see from a far off place and that not allowing me to get in will defeat the very purpose.

Sometimes youngsters with backpacks get in. With the i- phone in the ears, a hand held device with which they are perpetually messaging, it is indeed anybody's guess as to the fate of the person standing right behind this youngster. He will have to cave in and adjust.

It is amazing to see fit looking people wait long and use lift to climb 1 flight of stairs up or down. Worst case scenario is when a person wanting to go from the 1 floor to the ground floor gets in as the lift climbs from the 1 floor upwards.

It is not as if nothing interesting happens inside a lift. Many calls are made, messages are sent, decisions are taken and perhaps bonds are forged. There was a rumor that a young doctor proposed to his sweetheart kneeling down with a red rose in the lift at midnight as the lift went up from the ground floor to the 10 floor(ICU). I am not sure what the result was.

One of the most important decisions in connection with the starting of our alma mater is supposed to have taken place in the lift. Dr. TMA Pai, the visionary who built the KMC was finding it difficult to get an university affiliation for the college. He went to meet Dr. Laxamansami Mudaliyar (who was the vice chancellor of the Madras university) who just would not give him an appointment. Not the one to be defeated easily, Dr. Pai patiently waited for many days. He found out that Dr. Mudaliyar would be alone when he went home down the staircase after the days work. He decided that it would be the best time and one day got in with Dr. Mudaliyar. Before the lift reached the ground floor, Dr. Mudaliyar was so impressed with Dr. Pai that he went up again to his office and invited Dr. Pai to join him. The rest, as they say, is history!

I am also reminded of a horrible episode when one of my patients who was staying in a new building (still being completed), went into the lift hole (which he imagined to be a lift) and fell into the basement sustaining a fracture. He shouted for his servant to help him who in a state of confusion as how to help his boss, voluntarily jumped into the lift hole causing a second fracture for the bass and one for himself! The boss was lucky to be alive!

DO NOT FRET OVER REJECTION - STANFORD UNIVERSITY WAS BORN DUE TO A REJECTION!

Everyone has undergone an experience of a rejection sometime or the other. Maybe more often than once. Usually one tends to get upset and give up. Today I want to tell a story of how a great university was born out of an unreasonable rejection.

Mrs and Mr Stanford - the lady in her faded gingham dress and the man in a homespun threadbare suit went timidly to Boston without an appointment to meet the President of the Harvard university. After all, their son who was studying at the Harvard University had suddenly died and being grateful (as he was very happy as a student) they wanted to contribute something to the university as a memorial. The secretary gave them a surprised look and felt that the president had no time for such "country hicks". He never bothered to convey to the president their desire to meet him. He would not be interested anyway. Then he faced a strange problem. They would not go away! He had to find a way of getting rid of them.

The secretary reluctantly approached the president and appraised him of the situation. "They will leave only after seeing you" he said. The president very reluctantly agreed to meet them only for a few minutes. "My son attended Harvard for a year and he was very happy. He got killed accidentally. We have come to see you and offer to build a memorial for him Harvard.". The president was surprised. What kind of a memorial these "country hicks" could afford anyway? He simply told them that was impossible. "We could not erect a statue for each person who died while studying at Harvard. Then this place would look like a cemetery." "Oh no, not a statue. We were thinking of giving a building". The president got visibly annoyed. "Do you know how much a building costs? All our buildings cost more than seven and a half million dollars!". The lady was silenced. She thanked the president and the couple left.

As they walked out, the lady asked her husband "Is that all it costs to start a university? Why not start one on our own?" Now it was the president's turn to be bewildered. The couple travelled to Palo Alto, California, and established an university bearing their name - the Stanford University - a fitting memorial to their son the Harvard university no longer cared about.

The lesson to be learnt from this story is never to judge some one by the appearance. To be able to judge some one's character and abilities one has to spend quality time and listen to them. Only after a tactful communication, one try to can judge the other person

Next time someone rejects you do not feel offended. Maybe that will be a foundation for a greater achievement!

SERENDIPITY - ITS ROLE IN THE DISCOVERY OF PENICILLIN

Serendipity means a «fortuitous happenstance» or a «pleasant surprise "Horace Walpole 1754). It was made in reference to a Persian fairy tale about 3 Princes of Serendip (Ceylon) "who were always making discoveries by accidents and sagacity of things they were not in quest of". Serendipity had a role to play in many scientific innovations. Discovery of Penicillin and Microwave oven (Percy Spencer 1945) are 2 examples.

The days story is about the discovery of Penicillin aided by serendipity and a chain of people with tenacity and good observation. However, the major credit went to the person who started it all, Sir Alexander Fleming who discovered Penicillin in 1928. When this 'careless' lab technician returned from a 2 week vacation a mold had developed on an accidentally contaminated staphylococcus culture plate. He also noticed that this mold had prevented the development of staphylococci. It had effects only against gram positive strains. He is reported to have said "One sometimes finds what one is not looking for. When I woke up just after dawn on September 28 1928, I certainly did not plan to revolutionize all medicine by discovering the world's first antibiotic, or the bacteria killer. But I guess that was exactly what I did." Fleming stopped studying penicillin in 1931. Howard Flory and Ernst Chain continued the research at Oxford. The landmark work began in 1938 when Florey and Ernst Chain produced a series of crude fluid penicillin extracts. 50 mice which were seriously ill with staphylococcal septicaemia were promptly rescued in 1940. In 1942, Ann Miller became the first civilian patient to be successfully treated with penicillin

At that time the problem was of continuous availability of the drug. Albert Alexander police constable who was ill with staphylococcal sepsis responded well to penicillin but died after 5 days of initial improvement due to non availability of the drug. In 1941, Florey went to Peoria in the US with Heatley (a biochemist) to study means of mass production of penicillin. They realized that Penicillium notatum would never yield desired quantities of Penicillin. Mary Hunt, a lab assistant picked up a cantaloupe at the market covered with a "pretty, golden mold". Serendipitiously the mold turned out to be Penicillium chrysogenum which would yield 200 times penicillin as compared to P. notatum. With mutation causing technologies and radiation, the yield of penicillin was increased 1000 fold.

The acid test for Penicillin came in the form of Second World War. If the drug was indeed good, the mortality due to sepsis should come down substantially. That is what exactly happened. The mortality due to sepsis as compared to the first world war (18%) came down substantially to 1 % during the second world war. Penicillin was made. It had come to stay.

The story has a not so good ending. In 1945, Fleming, Florey and Chain were awarded the Nobel prize. Heatley was left out. In 1990, Oxford made up for this oversight by awarding Heatley the first honorary doctorate in its 800 years history.

Is there a word with the opposite meaning as serendipity? Yes, there is. It is called Zemblanity (William Boyd). It means "making unhappy, unlucky, and expected discoveries occuring by design". This term meaning an "unpleasant surprise" is derived from Nova Zembla, a cold, barren land with many features opposite to Serendip (Sri Lanka).

The search for the first antibacterial drug was greatly aided by Serendipity. It was not done for financial gains. Current research for newer antibiotics which is done keeping in mind the possible financial returns is rightly greeted by Zemblanity!

THE STORY OF ROENTGEN'S DISCOVERY OF X RAYS - A MEDICAL MIRACLE THAT UNSETTLED PHYSICS AND HELPED MEDICINE!

Today's story is about the discovery of one of the most fascinating things in Medicine - the X Rays.

In the winter of the year of his 50th birthday, an year after his appointment to the leadership of the University of Wurzberg, Rector Wilhelm Conrad Roentgen noticed a barium platinocyanide screen flourescing in his laboratory as he generated cathode rays in a Crookes tube some distance away. 3 days before Christmas, he brought his wife to the lab and took an image of her hand. It revealed bones of her hand and a ring. On the 28th December, he delivered the news of his discovery to the Wurzberg Physico-Medical society. On 4th January the news was relayed to the Berlin Medical Society from where the world press picked it up. On the 13th January he was awarded the Prussian order of the crown. On the 16th January the New York Times announced the discovery as a "new form of photography capable of transforming medicine by revealing hidden foreign bodies"!

The public and the physicians were equally enthralled by the discovery. It shook the entire foundation of Physics and the Physicists had to change their views on what was till the believed to the gospel truth. The research on the 'cathode rays' continued. Meticulous research by a German scientist, Philip Leonard inspired Roentgen to see that the rays described by him traveled much farther than the cathode rays.

The Humor Magazine, Punch, gave a poem. I have reproduced a stanza here:

> O, Roentgen, then the news is true,
> And not a trick of idle rumor,
> That bids us each beware of you,
> And your grim and graveyard humor.

Though Roentgen himself produced only 3 papers in the field, others jumped in. The X rays were used to locate the bullets; find out breaks in the bones. Dr. Henry W Cattell an anatomist in Pennsylvania used it to demonstrate Kidney Stones and 'cirrhotic livers'. In 1896, X rays were used to study human heart and brain(?). Vietnamese mummies and a new born rabbit were x rayed in 1896. In the same year, a German doctor used X rays to diagnose sarcoma of the tibia in a young boy. In 1897, hair loss and skin burns were identified as side effects. Roentgen now got interested in the physics of the X rays and was seriously interested in holding a position in theoretical physics a newly emerging German field.

Other industries also started using X rays - the Shoe industry made it a custom to study the bones of the feet to select the best suited shoes. The fashion industry wanted to satisfy the curiosity of the people by finding out the material used in the stilettos and what the model wore under her dress! The steel industry used it to test the strength of steel. Needless to say the maximum utility was found in the medical indications. Antonie Beclere of France in 1906 used x rays to study the stomach. Soon the x rays were used to treat cancer.

Now an interesting anecdote - 100 years after the discovery of X rays, a x ray machine was found at the Maastricht University Medical Center in the Netherlands by Gerrit Kemerink. Using that machine he took an image of the hand. The process took him 90 minutes as against 20 milliseconds for the new machines! The radiation dose needed was also 1500 times more explaining the frequent effects of hair loss and skin burns that used to happen!

DOCTOR AS A DETECTIVE - THE ART OF GETTING AT THE ROOT CAUSE BY SIMPLE OBSERVATION - IS IT A DYING ART?

A young girl consulted me yesterday. She had come for a general check up. Routine history revealed menstrual irregularity. Her build, dietary habits suggested a possibility of Polycystic Ovarian Disease. On close questioning she said she was on treatment for acne and' migraine.' I asked for an abdominal ultrasound (which indeed revealed Polycystic Ovarian disease) serum Prolactin level which promptly came as high. The diagnosis was obvious - Pituitary tumor most likely prolactinoama. One must make use of the opportunity and see whether one diagnosis is possible. Patient gives a story. Doctor must listen to it patiently.

I remember the good old days where the skill of observation was taught as one of the first things. One of our professors ordered a student to exactly mimic him.

The professor dipped a finger in a jar of urine and then into his mouth. The obedient student did just though he felt repulsive. The Professor had a hearty laugh. "I dipped my middle finger in urine and put my index finger in my mouth! You should have observed!" he said. Students had their first demonstration of 'skill of observation'.

A keen sense of smell was a prerequisite for a good physician. Ability to smell ketone bodies is an asset. It has helped me many times to start treatment before the urine report arrives. One of my professors in surgery could smell malaena from quite a distance. "You learn the trick once and you will never forget it" he would say. So true!

I remember seeing a patient at home for abdominal pain and vomiting many years ago. A just married girl just back from honeymoon was lying quite ill in a room near the window. She was writhing in pain. I observed urine kept nearby indicating her inability to use the toilet. The sunlight was directly falling on it and the urine had a port wine color. The diagnosis was made on the spot "Acute Intermittent Porphyria". I was a beginner at that time and I discussed with my chief. He gave me the 2nd clue for the diagnosis. "When a good surgeon thinks that the abdominal pain is due to a medical cause after ruling out surgical conditions, and when the physician thinks it is a surgical cause after ruling out medical conditions, think of Porphyria".

I once visited a young relative of mine, an orthodox girl who had just got married. She was having high fever and loose motions. I was thinking of the possibility of Typhoid. Just then she developed a rigor so typical of Malaria. On looking beneath the bed, I observed stools typical of Amoebic dysentery. I was indeed surprised at the obvious diagnosis of Intestinal Amoebiasis because she had not eaten any external food. How did she get it then? I promptly referred Manson's Textbook of Tropical Medicine. There it was- Acute Falciparum malaria can sometimes unmask Amoebic cysts (the quiet forms) and result in mass excystment resulting in a fresh attack of intestinal Amoebiasis without fresh infection.

We had a Professor who was an excellent teacher. He was good in bedside teaching. He would attract a lot of students by his dramatic classes. He would demonstrate clinical findings accurately and at the end of the class ask for the chest x ray. The students would run to the radiology department and get it. It would exactly match with his clinical findings! One day a PG student volunteered to guess the findings on the x ray. Much to the surprise of the students he was right. The professor was flabbergasted. "How on earth did you guess?" he asked the student. in desperation. The student gave a wide grin and said "Sir, I saw you go to the radiology department just before the class. I went in and saw the x ray too after you came out!"

MEMORIES FROM CLINICAL TRAINING - WHEN MURMUR WAS MUSIC TO THE EARS!

Being a clinical student was considered the turning point of the career of a medical student. This enabled him to obtain 2 status symbols - a stethoscope and an apron. The first day as a clinical student was a great feeling. Finding out the posting, locating the ward and finding out who are the teachers were the main tasks. Fortunate few posted in Medicine would be having a chance to join the clinics and get a ring side view of the happenings (literally!). The Professor taking the class at the bedside would be flanked by the students of the final postings. Around them would be the students from the middle postings. Located peripherally would be the 'freshers' forming the outer circle. They usually got to see the backs of the seniors and listen to their discreet comments made under the breath (about the professor). They would be eagerly waiting for a chance to listen to the heart murmur.

Without this their life would be incomplete. Those who got the first chance to listen to the murmur would have to stand a treat to others. Still it was worth it!

On a particular day, we came to know that the next day's case would be one with a murmur. The news was leaked by the nurse who in the first place told the senior students about it. We came to the ward ahead of time and tried to hang around the patient only to be shooed by the senior students. They were surprised to see us and we feigned ignorance. As expected the professor came and the class was taken. When the time came to discuss the auscultatory findings the professor agreed that there was indeed a murmur. He wanted all students to listen in by turns. We were thrilled. We heard the 'Machinery murmur" a variety of continuous murmur. Then we were told the synonyms - train in the tunnel murmur, rolling thunder murmur, cartwheel murmur, humming top murmur, churning murmur, mill wheel murmur. We became the eyesore to the other students. The next day one of our batch mates called a girl from another batch to demonstrate the murmur to her mainly to impress her. As the process was in progress, the professor walked in and silently watched the scene. He politely interrupted "My dear boy, you have all markings of a potential good teacher. But remember, the ear piece should be in your ear when you auscultate for the murmur. The boy was so ashamed that he did not turn up for the class for the next 2 days!

Hearing the first murmur, hearing the briut over the carotid / aorta/ renal artery for the first time are unforgettable events. We got reprimanded for looking for them in the wrong place. I rejoiced the moment I picked up a bruit on the skull. I would never forget the moment I heard a bruit over the eye with exophthalmos.

Sadly the doppler and echo have become "killjoys" of Clinical medicine depriving the students of the rightful thrills involved in the learning process. I agree these modalities have made the testing more objective but it was the subjectivity and vulnerability that made us more efficient! These are the things that made a teacher important. No doubt the teaching goes on. The pleasure derived in the process of teaching (by the teacher) and the process of learning (by the student) are as important as the learning process itself. I am afraid this and the stethoscope - the earlier status symbol of the clinical student are on their way out!

WHEN FALCIPARUM MALARIA CAME BACK TO MANGALORE - AN AMAZING STORY!

Sangeetha came to visit me yesterday with her mother. Ready smile, cheerful personality reminded me of her father, my god friend, Dr. Vaidyanathan, my contemporary, who was a specialist doctor at the city corporation of Mangalore. Unfortunately he is no more. Sangeetha is his daughter who is a HR Professional and is doing well for herself. During the course of our interaction, I told her a story She was thrilled. I will now tell you that story.

One of my professors used to take 3 three hour classes at the bedside on Malaria. We had to stand. for the entire duration. The professor was a gold medalist from the London School of Tropical Medicine and also from the Calcutta School of Tropical Medicine. No one had the courage to ask him why 9 hour class is needed when the disease is never seen in the country! One day, a student asked him that question. "When your city gets Malaria, there will be no one with the first hand knowledge of Malaria. Even this much information will prove to be inadequate!"

This proved to be prophetic when the event happened in mid 80 s. I saw a 24 year old boy having classical 'malarial rigor'. I had never seen one earlier. I was thrilled. I sent him to the lab for the blood test - P smear for Malaria. I got a phone call from the lab saying that it was positive for Falciparum parasites. I was in the clinic. I left everything as it is and ran to the lab. I saw the gametocytes which were banana shaped. I wanted to scream and tell the whole world I had seen a positive smear for Falciparum. I wanted to learn all that is there and teach my students. I even took a peripheral smear to show them!

Next day, I got up earlier than usual. I went to the hospital. Took a class for the students. They were also thrilled to see the peripheral smear. After the class I proudly went to the Dt. Malaria Officer. After all, I was the first doctor to see the parasite. Imagine my surprise when I was rudely shouted at and shown the door. "The whole thing is a figment of your imagination, he roared, this is a simple vivax infection!" Do not spread rumors!" I felt very bad. Next I went to the DHO. A worse fate awaited me here. "So you are the rumor monger. Do you know how much work is there if Falciparum is detected. Forget you ever saw it!" he said. I went home crestfallen.

Two weeks later, I got a frantic phone call from my lab. "We are finding a Falciparum positive in a VIP! What shall we do?" I insisted on the correct reporting. That evening the DC called a special meeting and declared officially that there was indeed Falciparum malaria in Mangalore. I was curious to know who was the VIP. To my utter surprise, it was my friend Vaidyanathan's wife- Sangeetha's mother. I barged into his office and said "How is it that your wife is more important than a common man?" He patiently listened and consoled me with his trademark smile "Dear Raghavendra, it is the DC who thinks my wife is important because he is my friend. I understand you. All are important. In fact, you should be happy - they have finally accepted the presence of Falciparum malaria in Mangalore" I was happy too!

When I ended the story Sangeetha flashed the trademark smile and said "Incredible story, uncle". Incredible indeed. For a moment I thought it was a mirror image of my friend Dr. Vaidyanathan!

A TALE OF TWO PROFESSORS - BOTH WERE BRILLIANT; WHO WAS SMARTER?

In the sixties and seventies, there were 2 professors - both brilliant, both were highly qualified academically. Both were gold medalists from London school of Tropical Medicine and Calcutta School of Tropical Medicine. Both were excellent teachers.

One was a clinician with a highly successful private practice. The legend had it that he saw a patient anywhere - in the market, in a hotel, on the corridor and was very popular. The other professor was witty, with a sense of sarcastic humor. Both were good clinicians with good diagnostic skills. The popular professor had studied at Rangoon.

The popular professor took classes after making sure sufficient students have assembled. If he felt the numbers were not sufficient, he would make the patient sit or stand on an elevated platform so that more people got to see and would get attracted and attend. He would discuss loudly.

The findings existent and non existent would be discussed and his unit PG s would endorse the same. The whole drama was very impressive as well as very educative. The sarcastic teacher on the other hand would take precise, concise, accurate classes. His sarcastic sense of humor would drive the not so intelligent students away. But the classes were highly appreciated. The same case would be presented twice - the sarcastic professor would diagnose Amoebiasis (his favorite diagnosis)and the popular doctor would diagnose Cardiac failure (his favorite diagnosis) and students got to learn 2 diseases!

Then the popularity with the medical representatives. The popular doctor was their darling. He would oblige them with ready prescriptions. The sarcastic doctor would ask complicated questions at the end of which no prescriptions would follow unless he was thoroughly satisfied about the need and the quality of the drug. The distance to which he threw the bottle or the tablets was inversely proportionate to the quality of the drug! The legend has it that a satisfied patient of his, an owner of a pharmaceutical company formulated Diethyl Carbamazine Citrate syrup to his specification for the treatment of Tropical eosinophilia.

Then there was the Grand Rounds. Grand rounds was the ultimate event - a sort of show of strength - The chief accompanied by assistants, PG students, Interns, UG students, and students from other units would walk the long corridors together discussing various patients and other clinical problems. One group would have to cross the other person's wards where the group would intentionally slow down and have a show of a discussion. Sometimes they (unintentionally)met on the corridors with their respective groups resulting in verbal fireworks! In one such episode, the popular professor asked the sarcastic professor "I am sorry to hear that your son failed II MBBS exam. What happened? Was he not smart enough?" The sarcastic professor was enraged. He coolly said "Thanks for the concern, professor. It is not that he was not smart enough. If that was the case professor, I would have sent him to Rangoon for his studies!"

The aftermath - The son of the popular professor went on t become a cardiologist and settled abroad. All the 3 sons of the sarcastic professor became doctors and settled abroad. He died of cardiac failure and arrhythmias believing all along he was suffering from Amoebiaisis!

CAN COMMON LOW COST DRUGS BE USED TO TREAT CANCER? WHY THEN THERE IS NO HYPE ABOUT THESE?

Cancer is an expensive disease. Investigations and management cost a lot of money. Insurance does not help much unless one knows the exact method of extracting that from the insurance companies. Availability of inexpensive drugs is the dream of many patients. It would be even better if drugs which are inexpensive and are already being used for other common diseases can somehow be useful for the treatment of cancer. I am talking today of exactly this scenario. I am sure these facts will leave you dumbstruck and seething with anger against the commercial nature of the pharmaceutical industry.

METFORMIN is the first drug I am addressing. Everyone knows Metformin. Doctors use it for Diabetes, Cosmetologists for obesity, Gynecologists for PCOS. It is a cheap drug with high safety profile and low cost. It is synthesized from French lilac and is found to limit the recurrence of particularly prostate cancer and early breast cancer. In fact, the National cancer Institute of US and Canadian Health services have joined hands for a large clinical study. Interestingly the way it works is by reducing the supply of excess glucose to the cancer cells (on which they thrive) and also affecting the mitochondria within the cells. It has even demonstrated promise in killing chemotherapy resistant cancer stem cells.

The next wonder drug is CIMETIDINE. This H2 receptor blocker in fact is an OTC drug. This is shown to halt tumor growth when used in conjunction with the standard chemotherapy. It seems to work well in cell culture in human and animal studies. Benefit is seen in Colorectal cancer. It also showed a statistically significant improvement in overall survival.

The next magic drug is NITROGLYERINE. Originally created to make explosives, it has been in use for more than 130 years mainly for the angina pectoris Used in conjunction with the standard chemotherapy, it has shown to it has been shown to improve the response of many cancers including that of the lung and prostate.

The next promising group of drugs is BETA BLOCKERS. Regularly used in the treatment of hypertension and arrhythmias, it has been shown to control the growth of a wide range of cancers, including those involving the breast, bowel, ovary, lung and melanoma. Lab studies have shown promise in the inhibition of progression of the breast cancer and metastasis. Animal studies showed promise in the response to chemotherapy. Human studies showed promise in the decrease of progression of ovarian and pancreatic cancers. These benefits were seen with Propranolol, Atenolol, Metoprolol.

The last drug I am going to name will leave you really surprised - It is a commonly used humble deworming agent, -an antiparasitic drug MEBENDAZOLE! When used in in conjunction with the standard chemotherapy, it is found to reduce the tumor growth. It is found to help in the treatment of Brain and Adrenocortical cancers. It has also shown promise in metastatic adrenocortical and metastatic colon cancers. However, no human studies have been completed upto now.

The question therefore arises, if these drugs are indeed good, then why there is no focused research going on? Why serious attempts are not being done to exploit this knowledge to the benefit f the mankind? One does not have to be an Einstein to guess the answer. There is no monetary returns for the research / clinical trials / clinical usage of these drugs. Unless carefully planned studies are conducted, these drugs will be soon shoved to the corner and made invisible to the doctors and patients!

THE UNFORGETTABLE MANIPAL GLOSSARY!

No one ever forgets their life at Manipal. Most memorable is the Manipal Lingo. The special terms we used there. I will share some of those that I recollect.

"IST" - Indian Standard Time - to denote the delay in the arrival for an appointment or a class. Sometimes shortened to IT - Indian Time.

"No probs"- When a desperate friend asked "can you lend me ten rupees?" an equally desperate friend would answer "no probs - only wait till the month end!"

Grandfather's road" - Usually mused by a motor bike rider to the pedestrian coming on the way "You think this is your grandfather's road, hah?"

"Gone case" - Irredeemable / Irretrievable - "You are a gone case man, no attendance, how are you going to appear for the exams?"

"Fierce" - Terrific / Fantastic - usually used for a good looking girl- "Boy, that girl, sure fierce man; looks like Marylyn Monroe"!

"Double headed snake" - Untrustworthy / Sneaky - "He is a double headed snake, damn, he stirs up trouble by carrying tales between both the parties"!

"Down the valley" - Along the sloping road to Parkala- usually used to denote booze joints - "Hey, exams are postponed; we shall go down the valley and celebrate!"

"Joint" - That is a tricky one with multiple meanings - In Anatomy - A movable junction between 2 bones; In common parlance "An eating place- that joint is no good, man!"; In the last usage "A rolled up paper or a cigarette containing Marijuana -have a joint I just rolled up one!"

"Grass" - Multiple meanings - Grass of the KMC greens / vegetables. "He is a grass eater, man!"

"Cherry" - A fruit - rarely used in that sense ; A good looking girl -" can I borrow your Brut, got a date with a cherry tonight!"

"Fag" A slang commonly used for a cigarette

"Pain in the ass" - Somebody being a nuisance - a painful situation about which nothing much can be done! "He is a pain in the ass, man!" Almost an equivalent is "Pain in the neck" which is less disturbing!

"Heights" - The ultimate level of something "Heights of stupidity - a real moron- half the students were described so! Heights of Insanity - word used to describe the other half of the Manipal students!

"Bug" - A small unpleasant insect - a term used to denote persistent disturbance or irritation.

"Take off" - To run away - "We got 3 holidays in a row, let's take off to Bangalore, man!"

"Tube light" - A person taking a long term to understand simple things. "You are a real tube light, man!"

"Solid"-- Very good / Fantastic / Terrific" "Hey, that girl is solid, man!"

"Grub" - Rarely used to denote its true meaning (insect larva) - food / chow "Lets have some grub in the mess, man!"

"Crash out" - Go too bed usually to sleep undisturbed - "Forget the movie tonight, man, I am going to crash out!"

"Thengah" Used to denote a dumb person "You are a real tengah, man! You dont even know the way to the Manipal Power Press!"

"Lah" A staunch Malaysian word - Cant be defined ; but used with some other word, emphasises what is being said. "I can't come to thew movie, lah; I want to sleep, lah, verry sorry lah!"

"Dah" - Another typical Malaysian word- probably indicated darling(?) - No, dah, I can't come; Please lend me your notes, dah!"

"UFO" - A powerful word meaning "get lost fast" - "UFO dah, I don't want you in this room!"

"Wah wah" A word usually used to indicate extreme sarcasm / mockery

"Check the scene" - to verify - "check the scene and tell me whether he is there!"

"Kachang, lah" Another Malaysian term used to denote making a task sound easier than it really is - A senior telling a junior (encouragingly) - Just study the tracts, lah, its kachang lah, you can surely do it!"

"Vie" - A slang for "to go". "Let's vie for a movie, man!"

"Got contact" - Know the right people in the right places - "Do not worry about the attendance lah, got contacts lah!"

"Crap" Rubbish / Nonsense - "boy, you must be nuts to read crap like that!"

And finally our all time favourite – "Long time no see lah" - applies to most of us now as we have not met each other for long!

I hope you traveled back in Time Machine and lived a slice of life in Manipal once again in the same old days!

Congratulations!

THE PRICE THAT SERVETUS PAID FOR DISCOVERING THE SCIENTIFIC FACT AND TELLING THE TRUTH!

"He who really understands what is involved in the breathing of man, has already sensed the breath of God" proclaimed the 16th century Spanish theologian and physician Miguel Servetus. Through the study of anatomy, Servetus sought rational explanation for the Bibilical passages placing the man's soul in the blood. He wondered how the breath of God reach the blood?

In 1553, he published his last work, the treatise Christianity Restored containing a passage describing the path of blood from the heart to the lungs. Servetus had discovered the pulmonary circulation. In doing so, he challenged the wisdom of Galen whose doctrines had survived the Middle Ages to become dogma. Galen believed that the blood mixed with the air in left ventricle(which he believed reached the left ventricle from right ventricle through tiny pores in the midwall) to become "vital spirit" with the breath of God. We now know that this is not true - blood from the right side of the heart that is from the right ventricle goes to the left side through the pulmonary artery.

Servetus challenged Galen's then conventional view and said that the breath of God was produced by "another contrivance". He noted that the blood travelled from the right side of the heart to the left side by the way of a "lengthened passage through the lungs in the course of which it is elaborated and becomes of a crimson color. He was literally describing the pulmonary circulation. "After mixing the blood became a fit dwelling place for the vital spirit" and finally entered the left side of the heart.

This fact was not observed. When William Harvey described the blood circulation 75 years later, he did not know of Servatus' work. The work of this Spaniard went unrecognized till about 1700 when an English surgeon discovered the passage. The theological doctrines declared heresy and Servatus had become a casualty of a religious battle.

It should be noted that Servatus lived during the period of Reformation, a period of religious ferment that led to the division of the Roman Catholic Church and the advent of the Protestantism.

Rebellious and outspoken, he published his first challenge to the church dogma at the age of 20. The work, however, opposed the fundamental doctrine of Trinity. This caused a furor resulting in Servetus fleeing from his house in Switzerland. He moved to Paris and studied Medicine under the pseudonym Michel Villanovanus. After his graduation, he became the physician to the Archbishop of Vienne. His interest in theology continued to dominate his life.

Theologist John Calvin at Geneva. was a prominent protestant reformer then. Hoping to get Calvin's approval, Servetus sent him a copy of his Christianity Restored. Contrary to his expectation Calvin was so outraged that he vowed to get Servatus executed if he ever set his foot at Geneva. Undaunted, Servatus got 1000 copies of his book printed in France under a false identity. However he was discovered, seized and handed over to the christian authorities. He knew that his fate was sealed. He somehow escaped during his trial.

He appeared in Geneva a few months later. Apparently, he was tempting the fate. Calvin had him arrested and put him on a trial for heresy. In the trial, he was found guilty of «infecting» his readers with «unhappy and wretched poison».

As the punishment, Servetus was burnt on stake on an October afternoon in 1553. A copy of his offending book was strapped to his waist.

I am sure you will agree Servatus was a true hero - he not only discovered the inconvenient truth but had the courage to go all the way to propagate it even if it meant death to him! Science progressed by the painstaking research and heroic sacrifices made by him and the likes of him!

THE GINGER JAKE PARALYSIS - ONE OF THE CLASSICAL MYSTERIES IN THE HISTORY OF NEUROLOGY - HOW IT WAS SOLVED?

In 1920, 18th amendment prohibited the sale and import of all alcoholic beverages. Attempts were made to produce legal alternatives to usual alcohol. A cottage industry started with this intention. Alcoholic extract of ginger was considered to be a patented medicine This liquid extract of Jamaican ginger was called "Jake" and could be sold legally.

To curb the abuse of Jake, a standard formula was defined for its manufacture (USP). The extract had to contain 5 grams of ginger per ml of the solvent. This resulted in a highly unpalatable bitter concoction. People were encouraged to mix this with soft drinks to make it taste better Agriculture department occasionally boiled the product and studied the extract in detail including the weight of remaining solids.

In order to make the product cheaper, alternative solvents were tried. Harry Gross, president of Hub products, used TOCP (TriOrthoCresyl Phosphate) thinking it is safe. Shortly after its release, thousands of people in Tennessee, Oklahoma, Kentucky suffered a mysterious disease manifesting as an ascending paralysis. An estimated 50000 people were stricken with paraparesis or paraplegia.

Dr. Epraim Goldfain was the first doctor to recognise it. In February 1930, he saw a man with a rapidly progressive foot drop. Within a short time he had 65 patients presenting with this mysterious affliction. Most of them were poor workers habitually consuming Jake. Working on this and other similar clues, the Maurice Smith and Elias Elvoe of NIH after analysing the samples determined that the toxic component to be TOCP These findings were confirmed by animal studies. Music industry picked it up and it went into 12 blues from 1928 to 1934. An United Victims Of Jamaica Ginger Paralysis was formed with 35000 members belonging to the poor class.

Later 105 people including 35 children died of Ethylene Glycol poisoning. Food, Drug and Cosmetics act was passed in 1938 to prevent any sale of medicines without safety testing. Die to weak laws, Gross got away without any Jail time till he again exported 640000 oz bottles to California after the ban He then served a 2 year jail sentence.

Symptoms of Ginger Jake paralysis developed in a week of the intake starting with the abdominal cramps, later involving the legs and then the paralysis ascended. Sensory symptoms and bladder involvement was rare. Some developed spasticity later suggesting a motor neuron involvement. Peripheral nerve and spinal cord were also seemingly involved

The Ginger Jake paralysis taught us a lot about other neurotoxins also. Organophosphate Induced delayed Neuropathy was picked up later. Thus TOCP could involve peripheral nerve (long fibres) and the spinal cord. The Ginger Jake tragedy was one of the largest mass poisonings in the history of neurology, many others were picked up later. These interesting cases included Peripheral neuropathy from Arsenic contaminated beer, Myoclonic encephalopathy mimiking Crutzfeldt - Jakob disease from GI preparations containing Bismuth; Encephalopathy and cerebral edema Triethyltin laced antibiotics to name a few.

Needless to say the Ginger Jake was withdrawn and the disease disappeared!

THE STORY OF A GIRL WHO WAS BEATEN BLACK AND BLUE BY HER FATHER - BUT WHY? HOW SHE WAS HELPED?

It was just an ordinary day. Those were the early years of practice when the patients were few and far between. There was this banker, a promising one at that. Professionally he was doing very well. He had 2 daughters. Normally all 4 would come together for any one's consultation. I thought it was a happy family.

That day they came for the elder daughter who was about 6 years old studying in the first standard. She was weeping. Body had bruises. It looked like she had been beaten black and blue. On inquiry, I was in for a surprise. She had been badly beaten up by the father! This was a delicate issue and I had to tread the path very carefully. I asked the mother how she sustained the injuries. She promptly replied that the father her reprimanded her for her poor scholastic performance. I was surprised. I asked her what she meant. She said that the girl was very backward in studies and stupid. This was an irritating factor for the father who was busy with his profession. When he came home after a hard day's work, mother would complain to him about the daughter. Her performance in school was awful. Tuition teacher had almost given up. She never finished home work. She hardly ever did anything right in the school. Teacher and the mother were very worried. Feeling irritated after a hard day's work, the father would lose his cool and beat her up real bad!

I decided to interact with the girl. She was shy. She was a bit reluctant to interact with me. After a little bit of coaxing, she opened up. I asked her name and she replied correctly. I asked her to write it. She tried but was all wrong. I asked her about alphabets and she could not answer - unusual for a 1st standard girl. I wrote an alphabet - she read it wrong. I have a bad handwriting. So I now wrote in big size capital letter and she was still wrong. I told her that the alphabet was A and asked her to name something starting with that alphabet. She said Zebra! Obviously wrong. Then I showed her some pictures and asked her to identify them. A house, a tree and the like. She could not. She was bad in repeating what was told. She could not recite even one nursery rhyme. I realized what the diagnosis was - Learning Disability - Dyslexia. Faculty of recognition of alphabets / pictures / numbers was all wrong. LBLD -Language Based Learning Disability could consist of calculation problems, reading problems, difficulty in auditory processing, repetition, and sometimes motor incoordination.

I took the parents into confidence. I explained to them what dyslexia was. I also told them that the child was not doing it intentionally. They were surprised. They still felt that the girl was beyond education and therefore stupid whatever the label was. She was a abnormal child and a academic liability. It took me a lot of effort to tell them that there is indeed a solution. She would have to be trained in a special school and would require personal attention and training there. They were a bit reluctant because they saw it as a means of segregation and also felt that the child would be marked as 'different from the rest' if she attended a special school. After counselling them and also sending them for special counsellers finally they agreed with the suggestion o send her to a special school. I am glad to say the girl improved a lot and did well for herself.

It is very interesting to note that children with these disorders get easily marked in an ordinary school. They manage well in their later life. Obviously the skills required for a career later are much less than those required in the years of schooling! The father went on to become a very successful a banker and held one of the topmost possible position in the banking industry just before his retirement. This also shows that skills of very fine understanding of human nature and man management are not really necessary to be an outstanding professional. They get easily overshadowed by the extraordinary professional skills!

WHY WERE THE CATS GOING ROUND AND ROUND AND COMMITTING SUICIDE AT THE MINAMATA BAY?

In 1956 cats in the Minamata bay walked around in circles, had convulsions, stumbled around, and seemed to commit suicide by jumping into the Minamata bay of Japan. This finding gave an early break in a series of patients with peculiar clinical features. What both the cats and the people had in common was that both ate the local fish. In 1956, a 5 year old girl developed what looked like encephalitis. 8 days later, her sister also developed similar illness. Altogether 54 patients were found to be suffering from Minamata disease. There were many similarities among these patients. Each one had eaten either fish or shell fish. Nearly all lived along the Minamata bay and were occupied in the fishing industry. Epidemiologists suspected the local fish as the cause but could not say why. To prove their theory, they brought cats from 100 miles away and fed them with the local fish. Same disease followed almost conclusively proving that eating the local fish was the cause.

To understand "why" we have to go back in time. In 1906, a small factory was established in Minamata by the Chisso corporation - a carbide plant for the production of Acetylene. Fertilizer production was also added in 1920. In 1951, the plant began manufacturing acetaldehyde for the used in plastics which involved mercury oxide as the catalyst. Inorganic mercury used was methylated in an acetylene reaction tank forming methyl mercury which was highly toxic. This had to be recycled. As the recycling was expensive, the company started to dump the waste directly into the bay. Locals and the fishermen complained. The silence of the fishermen's union was bought by paying the fisherman's union to keep quiet. More than 100 tonnes of mercury was deposited in the bay contaminating the water and the marine life within. Only in 1940, mercury as the toxin was seriously considered after a similar poisoning from a seed company in Britain.

The epidemiological research proved that the disease is not infectious or contagious. They said that dumping of the mercury waste was the cause and asked for a ban on fishing. Due to inaction, none of the recommendations were followed and many more persons also became ill. In 1968, another similar outbreak was seen in another town of Japan - Niigata due to water contamination at Agano River. The public became proactive and saw to it that the Chisso company halted the manufacture of acetaldehyde.

Minamata disease had 2 major victims - the patients who consumed contaminated fish usually in large quantities and their offspring. Clinical features included ataxia, incoordination, Paresthesias, constriction of visual fields, tremors, dysarthria. Autopsy revealed neuronal damage involving the cerebral cortex and the cerebellum. A variety of Congenital Minamata disease was seen with cerebral palsy like features at birth due to intrauterine exposure to toxic mercury. Mental retardation, limb defects, cerebellar ataxia, dysarthria, chorea microcephaly, hypersalivation were seen. The features developed 6 months after the birth reflecting the sensitivity of the developing nervous system. to the industrial toxins.

This episode taught us an expensive lesson - there are no shortcuts to waste disposal. Buying silence does not stop the effects of industrial pollution. This reflects the collective greed of the manufacturers, trade unionists and the society. More than 2 billion were paid as compensation which negated all the concealed illegal savings!

DOES THE GOOD THAT YOU DO COME BACK? MY EXPERIENCE IN HYDERABAD!

The occasion was a conference at Raichur. My colleague, myself and 2 lady doctors (both post graduate students) were travelling together. First lap of the journey was to Hyderabad by flight. It was a pleasant journey and was uneventful. We were supposed to reach Raichur by road - an Innova was arranged for the purpose. We had to wait for some time at the airport for the arrival of the vehicle. It was a new Innova.

After about an hour's delay, the vehicle reached us and we got into it.

The driver hit the road and was travelling at a speed of about 120 Km / hour when an unforeseen incident happened. It was a 8 lane expressway 4 lanes on the either side of a broad divider in the middle with plants planted in it. A huge truck was slowly travelling on the extreme right lane slowly. In fact, he should have taken the extreme left lane - but that is how the truck and the bus drivers drive with no rules followed and no civic sense. My colleague who was sitting in the front, turned back and started talking to me (I was sitting on the backseat). As I was speaking to him, I could see the road at the periphery of my visual field. I thought I saw a small dot which moved. To my horror, I suddenly realized that it was a human being. I saw it at a distance of about 2 KMs and it took us barely a few seconds to reach that area at that speed. He must have felt that we are far away and must have tried to cross the road. He came right in front of our vehicle, hit the windshield and was thrown off bleeding from the mouth, nose and ears and was deeply unconscious. We stopped our car. Reflexly, I knelt down to examine him for signs of life and to try to save him till he reached a hospital. After checking him for 3 minutes I found only a feeble pulse and no respiration at all. I frantically called the patrol police and they scoffed at my suggestion. I also realized that I was on the same road exposed to the same risk as the person who just died.

With nothing better to do, we stood at the roadside hoping for some vehicle to take us. To our bad luck, KSRTC buses were full and Andhra buses were running full. A burly gentleman stopped his car and held me by my arm and invited all of us to travel with him. He looked like a antisocial person but then, was the only hope for us. I persuaded my friends to get in. He promised to drop us at the next station. To our continuing bad luck, no vehicles were to be found in that place. He voluntarily took us to 2 more stations where the same fate awaited us. The he took us to a toll gate where all vehicles had to stop compulsorily.

He saw to it that we got in. We had to stand. We offered the 2 available seats to the ladies.

Then I asked him the million dollar question - why did he chose to help us? His answer was simple - you tried to help my man - all along risking your own life! He went on to add that we would have been promptly robbed of all our cash and valuables in the next 30 minutes by a gang of highway robbers. When I asked him how he knew all this, his reply was short and shocking. He was a reformed member of the gang! The person who died was a current member - a petty pickpocket!

Most of my professional career I worked at the Wenlock Hospital - drawing a salary 25% of what I would have had I worked in the corporate side. I enjoyed my teaching job and treating the poor patients. I think these poor patients bless us from the bottom of their hearts and the blessings do work. There were many instances in my life where I got this feeling repeatedly. I do not have any other explanation for the timely help that we got that day. Do you agree?

THAT'S MY DAD! - SOMETIMES I WONDERED WHETHER HE WAS TOO OFFICIAL!

I got a seat for MBBS in the First ever national level competitive exam held by the KMC in 1971. I was thrilled. I ran home and told my mother about it. When my dad came for lunch I excitedly told him too! He asked me how much it would cost. I said the donation would be 5000 and annual fees would be 1075 each year for 5 years. He congratulated me and informed me that I had to fund the donation myself and he would gladly pay the fees. I was shocked. I was a mere PUC pass and had no assets of my own. My only hope was my friend whose father was a Manager in the Canara Bank. I ran to him and explained the situation to him. He was very nice. But he did not have the required seniority for lending an education loan of 5000. He made a special trip to HO at Bangalore and did the needful. Just after that I qualified for a Government Merit Seat and got a seat at Mysore. I applied for a mutual exchange and fortunately it came through after some unexpected developments. The next stop was at the office of our founder - he used to meet everyone personally. He discussed the situation with me. I appraised him that there would be no donation if I took a merit seat and he also would have an extra seat at his disposal. He appreciated me (I was very touched by his gesture) and blessed me. I got my money back and settled the loan with the bank.

I was selected for the National Merit Scholarship after my SSLC based on my SSLC performance. I would get the scholarship till I completed my education. There was only one snag - Parent had to sign that the income was below a certain level. I happily went to my dad. His income was exact cut off value. He refused to sign saying that it was not BELOW the cutoff value. No amount of pleading worked. Then I used what I thought was the trump card - "If you do not sign, the offer would pass to the next boy and his father would sign and would get all the benefit even if the income is higher"! I said. "That, my boy," he said, "is the difference between his father and your father!".

When I joined MBBS, my friends told me I was 'safe' as he was a staff member. To my horror, he resigned the day I joined. He did not want any favors. He told me only 2 things. "1. Do not ask me to put in a word to anyone. I do not mind your failing. I will gladly look after you as long as you work hard. But no influencing. Achieve things if possible on your own. 2. I have a reasonably good name in the society. Do not do anything to tarnish it."

Just after passing the Rotary Club which he was a member of asked me to join. I told him about it. He immediately said - "I have a god name in the Rotary movement. Join only if you can follow all rules and stick to the timings. Otherwise wait till the time you can do these things and then join". I am still not a Rotarian!

Once I had to see a patient in a hospital. I said I will come at 2 o'clock. I had to drop my dad somewhere. He accompanied me and asked me to see the patient first. I reached the hospital at 2 15. I saw the patient and came back. He asked me "How many people were waiting with the patient?" I said "4". He immediately said "Then you have wasted 1 hour 30 minutes". I did not understand. He said 6 people including himself and me waited for 15 extra minutes which meant a total of 1 and a half hours was wasted. "Never do that again. Everyone's time is as precious as yours" he said emphatically. "If they are not there on time, you walk away".

PAUL DUDLEY WHITE - THE CRUSADING CARDIOLOGIST WHO GOT RECOGNITION FOR HEART DISEASE!

In 1911, Paul Dudley White entered Medicine. That was the year the heart disease was participating in the grim race with 2 better known causes of death - Tuberculosis and Pneumonia. In fact, he was one of the first specialists in Cardiology which till then was considered an insignificant field by his teachers.

Plunging into the study of heart diseased, he pioneered the use of Electrocardiograph - then a recently invented tool which recorded the activity of the heart by charting its electrical impulses. In 1914, he set up an ECG machine in the basement of the Massachusetts General Hospital. By 1931, he had collected 21,160 ECG s and case histories. By combining and analyzing this data, he wrote a 10000 page book on Heart Disease. It went on t become the standard textbook of cardiology for many decades.

He also studied the hearts of animals. He used the electrocardiograph to study the heart beat of animals. He found out that a larger heart beats fewer times than a smaller heart. The heart of a humming bird beat over 1000 times a minute where as that of a whale beat fewer than 15 times a minute!

He also realized that in the humans, the difference in the heart size could trigger significant variations of the heart beat which sometimes could be dangerous. He realized that the athletes could have enlarged, slowly beating hearts which could be essentially normal. He warned the other doctors about defining the 'normal' heart with too narrow a definition.

He became very well known among the doctors. In 1955, Eisenhower, the President of the USA suffered a heart attack while at office and White was summoned to treat him. He would report the daily progress to the people of the worried nation. He lectured to the country about the disease, its causes its treatment in a simple understandable language. This made him very famous with the public also.

White was a strong advocate of exercise. He was of the opinion that the labor saving devices and sedentary jobs made the Americans more prone to heart attack. He went on to declare "death due to heart attack before 80 is not God's will, it is man's will."

At the age of 75, he bicycled 30 miles per day. He used to say "people hold up their hands in horror that I do it!". But I hold up mine in horror that they don't!".

Finally he retired at the age of 86. Soon after, he suffered a stroke. While he was convalescing in the hospital where he had practiced for 58 years, a patient arrived and requested an examination by doctor White. The doctor obliged and examined the patient wearing a bathrobe.

Paul Dudley white lived his work and also loved it! He also thrived by it! He had a terse aphorism - "Hard work never killed any man!". He was a living example of that!

WOULD YOU ATTEMPT SOMETHING NEW WHEN EVERYONE RIDICULES YOU? - WERNER FROSSMANN'S VOYAGE TO THE HEART!

How many of us chose to think and act differently when almost everyone we know ridicules the concept? It requires a lot of courage to think and act ‹differently› in a scientific arena. Today I would like to narrate the story of Dr. Werner Frossmann who did exactly that. What happened to him makes an interesting and highly motivating reading!

Even as a student of Physiology Frossmann was a keen observer. He had seen an image of a man holding a rubber tube inserted into the jugular vein of a horse in an old French Physiology book in early 1920 s. This primitive picture left an indelible impression on the mind of this youngster for several years.

After his education, he became an intern at a small hospital outside Berlin. He suggested to his supervisors that such an experiment would be very rewarding if conducted and would give a lot of information about the heart. He went on to argue that this can be safely performed on man.

His supervisors summarily disagreed. They forbade his testing the procedure on a patient. Frossmann was determined. He offered an option. He said he would test it on himself! This offer was instantly refused. Nobody believed that he was right and that the experiment was safe.

Frossmann was made of a different stuff. He was certain that he was right and decided to try it out on himself with a secret experiment. He however thought that a vein in the arm would offer a safer route that a vein in the neck. With the help of another doctor, he anesthetized the crook of the arm, cut open a vein and inserted a slender rubber tube into it and asked his friend to push it forwards. The doctor who was helping lost his nerve midway and quit the experiment saying it was too dangerous.

In the summer of 1929, Frossmann tried it again this time with the help of a nurse. Hesitantly she helped him and guided him to the fluoroscope and held up a mirror so that he could see a shadowy image of his heart He watched the mirror and slowly advanced the tube to his heart. When he advanced the tube to 25 and a half inch, it entered the heart. He went into the X Ray room demanding a X Ray be taken. The technician instead ran out and alerted his colleagues. A well meaning doctor tried to pull out the catheter. Frossmann had to kick him a couple times on his shin to get him back to his senses. He tried the experiment 8 times in next 2 years and even injected a dye into his own heart on one occasion. He had done the first cardiac catheterization without realizing it!

Frossmann moved out to a small West German town of Bad Kreuznach and started to work there quietly. All of a sudden his work got recognized - he was awarded Nobel Prize for Medicine in 1956. along with American Cardiologists Andre Cournand and DW Richards. The sudden success left him stunned. He felt, remembering with pride, "like a village pastor who is suddenly informed that he has been made a cardinal!".

I wonder how many of us would proceed to prove a scientific fact on the face of a strong rejection? This is one example where one understands the importance of scientific reasoning and intuition over the current trend of "evidence based Medicine!"

THE STORY OF MICHAEL DEBAKEY - MENDER OF BROKEN HEARTS

Surgeons trying to mend broken hearts is a recent phenomenon. Michael DeBakey was one of the pioneering surgeons in this field which till then was much reared and respected by the surgeons. The reason for the hesitation of the surgeons was the fact that the same scalpel which could save lives would bring the patients close to death with a fine understanding of the subject and a series of bold steps, the Texas surgeon opened up the hitherto forbidden territory leaving a string of surgical operations to mark the way.

When DeBakey entered the medical school, arterial aneurysms(deadly bulges on the arteries) and the occluded arteries were thought to be the signs of impending death. Undaunted, DeBakey improvised surgical techniques by replacing the diseased portion of the artery with a strong, healthy graft.

Soon he realized that for a lasting success, he had to depend not on cadaver arteries but a more durable and a better substitute. He and his team tried many synthetic materials. Fianally in 1953, a machine was designed to manufacture what DeBakey exactly wanted. A seamless, knit, Dacron tube was born. The body was found to adapt remarkably well to the artificial arteries. New tissue would encase the synthetic tube, building in effect, new arteries.

These Dacron grafts broadened the horizon of the vascular surgeries. DeBakey could replace Aortic arches, give his patients new Abdominal Aortas, build Bypasses around hopelessly blocked arteries. He could bypass even the delicate coronary arteries. Whenever he could clear the coronary arteries, he used slips of the graft material to widen the arteries. He used these skills to ease the patients' suffering from narrowing of coronary arteries and carotid arteries (to help the stroke patients).

Naturally he became one of the world's foremost vascular surgeons. He now focused on the needs of the heart itself. He knew that the heart needed rest to recover from radical surgery. He found a solution in 1966. He implanted a device into the chest of a woman whose weak heart was adjusting to 2 newly implanted valves. After 10 days, the heart became strong enough to take over and the pump was removed. This success convinced DeBakey to build the ultimate gadget of his dreams - the artificial heart. was a possibility. He decided to wait for some more time so that some more research could be done. Thus he was a pioneer in the field of Coronary artery bypass surgery, Carotid endarterectomy and Left Ventricular assist device.

He worked in close association with Denton Cooley. Due to a misunderstanding, they fell apart. DeBakey wanted to postpone the first implantation of the artificial heart scheduled for 4 April 1969 due to a speaking assignment in Texas. Unfortunately Denton Cooley went ahead without his authorization and performed the surgery. However, they reconciled in 2007 and DeBakey invited Cooley for his Gold Medal ceremony and induced him into the Michael E DeBakey international surgical society. -In 1987 then President Ronald Regan awarded him the Presidential Medal Of Science.

In 2005 at the age of 97, he developed aortic dissection. Though he initially refused, the surgical team prevailed upon him and operated. After a series of complications and a 8 month hospitalization, he fully recovered and was grateful to his team! He died on July 21 2008 of unspecified causes.

In his lifetime he set an example for perfection. He regularly put in 24 hour days and worked tirelessly. He deeply mourned whenever a patient died. He used to say "You never get over that. Never!".

One patient put it thus "The 2 days I was privileged to put my heart in your hands, I learned what Blake meant - For mercy has a human heart and pity a human face!".

CASE OF THE "ANGRY TENANT" - WHY DID HE SHOUT AT THE LAND LORD EVERY MORNING?

This is a true story which happened at the beginning of my career. It was the golden era of medicine as the clinical medicine dominated and some investigations were available. The doctor who had good clinical skills was assured of work. However, one had to be meticulous and exhaustive.

Before getting a job in the medical college, I was working at a private hospital which had a good patient load. The owner of the hospital was also a land lord owning substantial land which was used for cultivation. His tenant was brought to the hospital and I was asked to examine him.

The complaint of the patient (tenant) was very peculiar. He would abuse and shout at the land lord every day. He was the main tenant, the leader of all workers. He was the key worker with whom the land lord had to negotiate for getting the work done. Usually such workers behave in a high headed manner. But the land lord would negotiate with them and settle the issue usually in his own favor. This tenant till recently was very respectful though his land lord had to bribe him sometimes to get his loyalty and keep him happy. Of late, he had become very arrogant. This obvious change in the behavior was noted by the land lord and the tenant was brought to me.

I saw him in the evening. He was courteous, smiling and willing to talk and willing to be examined. I found him almost normal. Only thing he told me was that he felt very very hungry in the mornings and lost his temper if the breakfast was delayed. When I went for work in the morning, a lot of people surrounded his room. I was told that he created a scene and was shouting and saying bad things about the land lord. This went on for some time. By then the breakfast arrived and he was visibly relaxed after that.

At first I thought that I was imagining things. But I was sure of my observation. I had to wait for one more day to validate the findings. The same scenario repeated the next day. I had arrived earlier to witness this myself. Indeed it was truly happening. The person who was sober in the noon, evening and night would flare up early in the morning - the transformation was genuine and reminded me of Dr. Jekyll and Mr. Hyde. Now that I had a lead to go be - abnormal behavior in the morning - I had to follow it and crack the case.

I had never seen such a case before. Then I tried to correlate the chain of events physiologically. The only difference in the morning as compared to other times of the day was hidden in that word - the event that made him almost normal - breakfast! On eating the first meal of the day, one was indeed breaking the FAST! This meant one thing - there was a connection between the fasting and the clinical features. The change behavior was precipitated by HYPOGLYCEMIA! Now I had to prove my hypothesis. Next morning I went to the hospital even earlier, and made sure I was there when the changed behavior happened. I drew the blood myself. That was sent to the lab for knowing the glucose levels. Lo and behold! The value was very low - something like 40 or so proving that hypoglycemia was indeed the provocating event.

My next objective was to prove the cause of low sugar which was happening spontaneously without any medicines known to produce it. I had read that retro peritoneal sarcomas can do it but had never seen a case to that effect.

I did some reading and found that some other tumors like hepatomas and uterine leiomyomas also did that. Those were easier to pick up clinically. The clinical examination was absolutely normal and therefore retro peritoneal sarcoma became the most likely diagnosis. Retro peritoneum is a hard place to examine bare handed. I was trapped in a cul de sac.

I did the next thing that was common at that time - ask the seniors for their opinion. They were very helpful. They agreed wholeheartedly with my line of thinking but warned me that I was speculating something that was very rare. Finally, I discussed the issue with the land lord who was also the owner of the hospital. I expected him to reprimand me for having thought of a rare possibility. To my surprise, he heard me out patiently, asked a few questions and said "I appreciate the reasoning and the logic. You have worked hard t crack the case. I am convinced you are right. I will operate tomorrow!". Needless to say, I spent a sleepless night.

The patient was promptly operated the next day. There was a tumor in the retro peritoneum. The biopsy report came as Sarcoma. The patient instantly recovered from the behavioral changes. I will never forget the case. More importantly, I will never forget the doctor's gesture of trusting a young doctor!

THE EPIDEMIC OF THE WITCHES' CURSE - WHY WERE HUNDREDS OF "WITCHES" IMPRISONED AND EXECUTED?

The place was Salem. The date 1692. The event - a tragic community event leading to the death of 20 innocent Puritans

In 1691, 8 teenage girls presented with altered behavior, gesturing, posturing, speech disorders, convulsive seizures - then known as "unknown distempers". A possibility of witch craft causing this was seriously considered. and this was even testified by the sufferers. 20 residents were tried and hanged for the offense. 150 more were incarcerated.

Some sought alternative explanation for these phenomena - mass hysteria, fraud, politics, social divisiveness were considered. It was noticed that the symptoms started after cold winters. This phenomenon was observed to have 2 presentations - Acute neurologic presentation - hallucinations, convulsions, paranoia, mania, sweating, spasms, jerks what we today refer to as acute Serotonin Syndrome. Chronic form was associated with Gangrenes of various parts of the body - Intense burning pain in limbs leading to (in severe cases)dry gangrene, black and mummified limbs which sometimes dropped off. Some women suffered spontaneous miscarriage.

Finally the phenomenon was traced to contaminated rye - the disease was Ergotism When this view was accepted, the new incoming Governor ordered the unconditional release of 150 incarcerated suspects.

Ergot thrived in cold winters followed by damp spring. Acute phenomena observed was really acute ergotism called by some neurologists as St. Vitus' dance (reserved by some only for Rheumatic Huntington Chorea). Chronic gangrenous ergotism was referred to as St. Antony's fire St Antony was a pious ascetic who lived in Egypt near Red sea. He fasted for long periods and used to have hallucinations. An order founded in France in 1100, took his name. They developed some treatment for the ergotism which seemed to work though the real improvement was probably due to consumption of a diet free of the contaminated grain. Sometimes the amputated limbs were left at the shrine as symbols of appreciation for cured patients.

Slowly the people noticed the vasoconstrictive and hallucinogenic properties of Ergot. Its use in labour was started in 1600 s though the acceptance came in 1900 s. The active substance useful in labor was isolated by Dudley and Moir in 1935 to be used IM or IV in PPH.

Though useful, the derivatives of Ergot Ergotamine and Dihydroergotamine have side effects - nausea, vomiting, abdominal pain, diarrhea, tingling and numbness, peripheral and coronary artery vasoconstriction. So Ergot derivatives should not be used in peripheral arterial disease, coronary artery disease, severe hypertension, stroke, pregnancy.

These drugs are metabolized in the liver by the enzyme cytochrome P 450 system. Any substance leading to a delay in its metabolism could precipitate r enhance the side effects. Macrolide antibiotics like Erythromycin, antifungals like ketoconazole, protease inhibitors used for HIV infections, antidepressants like fluoxitine can all result in this.

The experience with Ergot should have taught us to be more careful. Unfortunately it has not. We still find humans continuing to be victims of neurotoxins coming in from their own environment usually polluted by humans for the purpose of greed. - tainted products, drugs of abuse, contaminated bread, contaminated water and the like. Despite our knowledge, many of the sufferers and the causes must be going unnoticed and the perpetrators unpunished.

THE CASE OF THE "FROZEN ADDICTS" - WHY DID THE ADDICTS FREEZE? WHAT HAPPENED TO THEM?

Drug addiction is a serious thing. The extent to which an addict would go is decided by the desire, craving, knowledge and intelligence of the individual. He would go any length to procure the drug or even to manufacture it! This is the story of such ‹committed ‹ addicts!

Barry from Maryland spent some time in India with his family He initially bought the medicines from the street. One day in 1976, he took the drug manufactured by him intravenously. He felt severe burning at the site of injection and a sense of euphoria. Within three days he became immobile and mute. He was admitted to a hospital with a diagnosis of catatonic schizophrenia and was given phenothiazines to which he did not respond. He was promptly shifted to NIH where he was evaluated. Though the symptoms and signs closely mimicked Parkinson's disease, the suddenness of symptoms made them suspect a toxic etiology. Their research showed that he had tried to synthesize a chemical called MPPP (related to Meperidine). He inadvertently overheated the mixture and synthesizes MPTP instead. They had come very close to the answer. The next step was to try the hypothesis in the rats. They injected the rats with the same compound. Rats are not as susceptible to the toxic effects of MPTP and the catatonic phase seen was temporary. This resulted in a setback and the further research did not get priority. The issue became dormant.

In 1979, Barry's case was published. L Dopa was tried. He improved significantly and the speech returned. In 1978, he died of cocaine overdose. In 1982, George was found to have similar syndrome. He was also having extrapyramidal syndrome - Diphenhydramine did not work. He rapidly worsened and became stiff and immobile. He was later evaluated at Stanford.

William Langston tried to find a connection. MPTP seemed to damage the mitochondria of dopaminergic neurons. Dopamine reuptake blockers could prevent this damage. L Dopa gave temporary relief. Drug holidays prolonged the response but eventually the drug stopped working. Eventually a steriotactic implantation of fetal tissue was done in Lund, Sweden. This was tried in 2 patients George and Juanita and both did well.

The research showed that the compound, MPTP was like a bullet to substantia nigra resulting in immediate and long lasting damage. This compound gave an insight into the role of environmental causes in the genesis of Parkinson's disease.

The addicts had a very bad outcome. They became immobile and mute - truly "frozen addicts". Only some fortunate ones recovered. Others remained so for long periods.

The the case of the "frozen addicts" opened up a new chapter in the study of environmental toxins in the causation of PD. It also gave an insight into the animal studies in PD which is otherwise almost impossible due to the insidious onset of the disease! Thus the "frozen addicts" came as invaluable research tools!

HEIMLICH MANEUVER - LIFE SAVER FOR THOSE WHO CHOKE - DID HENRY JAY HEIMLICH REALLY DISCOVER IT?

Henry Jay Heimlich was born in 1920. He was a trained cardiothoracic surgeon He realized that choking was an important cause of death in the USA. He wanted t do something to save lives of those who had choked.

He was a keen observer. He had observed that abdominal thrusts helped the dogs to get rid of the material on which they had choked - that would dislodge from the throat and come to the stomach. He therefore attempted to try the same thing in the human beings - apply pressure on the chest and see whether the material blocking the throat would come to the stomach. Soon he realized that it was the pressure to the diaphragm that was really needed.

Heimlich suggested the use of a fist - placing the thumb against the patient's upper abdomen and grasping it with the other hand from the back with quick upward thrusts. He published the technique and its advantages in Emergency Medicine in June 1974. The article was titled "Pop goes the Cafe Coronary" Within weeks, he started receiving reports as to how the technique was saving lives. JAMA was so impressed with this technique that they renamed it as Heimlich Maneuver.

From 1976 to 1985, the American Heart Association and the Red Cross recommended guidelines on choking nicknamed as "the five and five"- 5 back slaps and if that failed 5 Heimlich Maneuvers. However in 2006 the term Heimlich maneuver was replaced by 'abdominal thrusts'. The drowning rescue guidelines regarded it as not only useless but also as potentially harmful because it could facilitate vomiting and choking on the vomit. There is no doubt that Heimlich Maneuver saved millions of lives.

Heimlich was not a one trick pony. He has contributed many other inventions to Medicine. In 1960 s he devised a simple inexpensive unidirectional valve in the Vietnam war which helped to remove blood from the chest of injured soldiers and saved thousands of lives.

In 1950 s he devised a surgery wherein he replaced the damaged part of the esophagus with a portion of the normal stomach in patients whose esophagus was damaged and resulted in the difficulty for the patient to swallow. He claimed that they were happy and could enjoy normal meals with the family.

In 1980 s he devised a Micro-trach, a transtracheal catheter to deliver oxygen more efficiently

Heimlich went on to claim that his technique would even help the patients with severe asthma. His adversaries however argued that though it helped remove blocked secretions, it did not help relief from the asthma in any other way.

His unusual experiment in China where he tried to induce Malaria -Malariotherapy- to therapeutically benefit patients with Lyme disease and AIDS by allegedly 'strengthening the immune system' was severely criticized and he was even labelled as a fraud by some.

His worst critic was his own son Philip Heimlich who later became the county commissioner of Hamilton County, Ohio, always held the view that the real discoverer of the maneuver was a doctor by name Henry Patrick and Henry Jay Heimlich only stole the idea from him!

Whatever the controversy may be, there is no doubt that the maneuver saved millions of lives. In 2002, George Bush, then the President of USA survived choking. Tennessee William, a Pulitzer prize winner who choked on the cap of an eye drop bottle and Marshall Subrato Mukherjee, India's first chief Air Marshall who choked on food in a Tokyo restaurant were not so lucky. Both died of choking!

THE STORY OF ROBERT KOCH - HIS FACE OFF WITH PASTEUR - DID KOCH REALLY DESERVE TO BE FAMOUS?

The disease Tuberculosis is as old as the mankind. It has been demonstrated in ancient Egyptian mummies (100 BC) and has found a mention in very old literature. Hippocrates called it Pthisis. It was a great killer rightly called the "captain among these men of death".

The possible infectious nature of the disease was speculated for many centuries. Hippocrates and Galen had suspected its contagious nature. Laennec was convinced that the tubercle was the common factor of all forms of tuberculosis. Schonlein gave it the name "tuberculosis" in 1839. Pasteur's germ theory in 1862 gave impetus to the research. Jean Antonie Villermin in 1862 proved that animals can get the disease from man by inoculation. Only demonstration of the causative agent remained. There was virtually a race among researchers to do this and finally in 1882, Robert Koch won the race!

On the 24 th day of March 1882, in the monthly meeting of the Berlin Physiological Society the formal announcement about the discovery of the tubercle bacillus was made. The meeting was chaired by DuBois Reymond and Helmholtz, Leoffler, Ehrlich and other medical luminaries were also present. There was no applause for the presentation though the audience must have sensed that this was going to be an important invention in the history of Medicine. The reason why it was not announced in the meeting of the Pathological society was because of the poor vibes Robert Koch shared with Rudolf Virchow, (Professor of Pathology), then a dominant figure in the Berlin Medicine. Robert Koch went on to further research in the field. He believed that the Tuberculin was the treatment of tuberculosis. Though he was proved wrong later, it became an important as a diagnostic tool in the management of tuberculosis.

Koch used Methylene blue as the stain. Culture proved to be difficult. Prof. John Tyndall of Londin used the term "Koch's bacillus" which was widely accepted all over the world. Erlich developed a method of staining which proved to be superior. In 1887, Ehlich tested his own sputum and found it to be positive! In a paper in 1884, he described what was later came to be known as Koch's postulates. Much earlier, in 1876 he had already described very virulent, spore forming Anthrax bacillus. He visited India in 1883 and identified Vibrio cholerae. During the second visit at the behest of the British government, he carried out important work on Bubonic Plague, proving that it was transmitted to the humans by the rat flea.

Robert Koch married his childhood friend Emily Fraaz in 1876. It was a happy marriage in the beginning and they had a daughter in 1878. However after 20 years of he married life, the relationship broke down and ended in a divorce in 1897. 2 months after the divorce, at the age of 50, he married a young actress Fraulein Freiburg who was only 21. The second marriage was followed by a social boycott and was forced to spend much time abroad.

In 1883, a controversy arose when Pastuer, calling himself 'second Jenner' tried to use methods of inoculation with the hope of preventing certain diseases. He used nasal discharge from horses who had supposedly died from horse typhoid and inoculated the rabbits with it. He used saliva from children with hydrophobia and inoculated the rabbits with it. When the findings were presented and discussed, Robert Koch took serious objections - the causative organism was not conclusively proved and the whole experiment was unsatisfactory. He claimed that the death of rabbits in both instances was due to septicemia. Despite all these shortcomings, Pasteur was considered a genuine "path breaker"

For all his discoveries concerning tuberculosis, Robert Koch was considered the father of scientific study of tuberculosis. In 1905, he was awarded the Nobel Prize in Medicine.

WHAT IS MUNCHHUASEN SYNDROME? WHO WAS MUNCHHAUSEN?

Every doctor has experienced patients who create symptoms or exaggerate them mainly seeking attention. They hop from doctor to doctor, hospital to hospital, producing thick charts, undergoing unnecessary admissions and even surgeries supposedly from a mental illness. This disorder has a name - Munchhausen's syndrome

Karl Frederic Munchhausen was a minor nobleman, a country gentleman with a large estate. He was born in 1720 and joined the Russian army and served there till 1750.

He returned to his home in Badenwerder. He has an extraordinary skill of story telling. He would tell terrific stories about his pole in wars and his other adventures mostly from his fertile imagination. Most of the events never happened or were greatly exaggerated. Rudlf Raspe in 1771 collected some of these cleverly put stories and published a book. He had to persue a series of lawsuits to protect his name.

The stories included some of these - An effect of storm in Ceylon; how he flogged a wolf(which had attacked him) till its skin turned inside out; Story of an extraordinary horse presented by Count Prozobossy with which he performs extraordinary feats and continues to do so even when the horse has been severed into 2 parts; A brass cannon travelling to the moon; building a bridge from Africa to Great Britain; How he sieged Seringapatam; His combat with Tippu Sultan and such other spooky tales

This condition differs from hypochondriasis and other somatoform disorders in that the patient does not intentionally produce the somatic symptoms. Emotional trauma during childhood or adolescence may be the contributing factors. In Arrhythmogenic Munchhausen, the arrhythmias are simulated. Munchhausen syndrome by proxy is a condition where the parent will ensure that the child will experience some medical affliction compelling the child to suffer the treatment and to spend a significant portion of the youth hospital hopping and doctor shopping. Some of them even undergo repeated surgeries simulating surgical illnesses.

In 1951, Richard Ashner published a paper in Lancet and titled it as Munchhausen's syndrome after this person. This was to give medical attention to this condition.

One has to suspect Munchhausen's syndrome when new symptoms keep cropping up every time a negative report comes. They are eager to undergo new tests, may have multiple surgical scars, history of visiting many doctors and many hospitals.

Baron Munchhausen became very famous. Books were written about him. Plays, and movies were made about his life. Illustrated comics were produced about his exploits. A puzzle/ hidden object game was produced which was named after him in 2012. In Russia, there is a club named "Munchhausen's grandchildren". Germany has arranged international tourism including the places visited by him. A museum was opened in his name where he had stayed with his wife. A commemorative coin was released by Latvian Central bank. In 1994 a main belt asteroid was named 14014 Munchhausen in honor of the Baron.

THE STORY OF HIPPOCRATES - DID HIPPOCRATES REALLY WRITE THE HIPPOCRATIC OATH?

Hippocrates known as the Father of Medicine epitomizes the Greek Medicine. His teachings in philosophy and medicine have influenced the practice of medicine through the ages.

He was born in 460 BC in the island of Cos. His father was Heraclides a physician, mother, Praxitela, daughter of Tizane. He had 2 sons - Thesallus and Draco and son in law Polybus. Polybus was his true successor. Hippocrates learnt medicine from his father and his grandfather

He is known well for some of his views. He was the first to say that the disease was due to natural causes and not due to God's wrath. The focus was on patient care and prognosis and not diagnosis. Another concept in the treatment of the disease was "crisis" the point at which the disease would abate or the patient would succumb to it. His therapeutic principles were humble and passive based on the nature's ability to cure.

He was known for his strict professionalism, discipline and rigorous practice He would always trim his fingernails and had a primitive operating room where he did splinting and minor surgery.

He contributed many things to Medicine. He is supposed to have written 79 books and 52 treatises - no body is sure how many of these were really written by him. He was the first to describe clubbing of fingers - sometimes called Hippocratic fingers. He described Hippocratic facies He gave very good descriptions of various diseases but did not name any syndromes. He gave the first description of Empyema. He devised a primitive speculum to study piles which must have been the first application of endoscopy He emphasized the importance of diet and exercise. He had the concepts of acute and chronic; endemic and epidemic; exacerbation, resolution, relapse and crisis.

The most famous contribution to medicine by him was the Hippocratic oath. which is a seminal document on ethics in medicine. It entails good medical practices and morals. It is controversial whether he wrote it at all!

Soranus of Ephisus, a Greek Gynaecologist of the 2 nd century was his first biographer. After him the famous physician was Galen who lived between 129 to 200 AD Thomas Sydenham, William Heberden, Charcot, William Osler followed his methods.

Hippocrates is also well known for some of his aphorisms - Gout never develops before puberty on men; before menopause in women and never seen in the eunuchs. - almost true even today. He probably described

Behcet's disease and Crohn's disease without naming them
He never spoke of a disease resembling rheumatoid arthritis
and so the disease must have been more recent!

Coins bearing his name and his profile were unearthed
from Cos. He is supposed to have died in Thessaly. A
sculpted head was found in the cemetary of Ostia which
bears a close resemblance to what is now accepted to be his
appearance

It is indeed unbelievable that a single person has
contributed so much to Medicine. No wonder he is liked,
loved, adored and admired. He definitely qualifies to be
called the "father of Medicine"

JEAN MARTIN CHARCOT - PIONEER IN NEUROLOGY - ALSO A PATHOLOGIST AND A RHEUMATOLOGIST - BEST KNOWN FOR HIS 18 EPONYMOUS CONTRIBUTIONS TO MEDICINE

Jean Martin Charcot is considered the father of Neurology. But he was much more than that. He was also a trained Pathologist. He was also interested in Rheumatology. He is considered to be one of the most influential physicians of all times.

He was born on 29 November 1825. His father was a cottage builder. Being better than his brothers, his father supported only him to pursue the higher education in Medicine. A keen observer, a good painter, he had a good visual memory. He was good in German, Italian and English languages.

He graduated from the medical school of Paris at the age of 23. He was an intern at Salpetriere hospital, Paris.

He held various positions at that hospital including Chef de Clinique(1853), Physician t the hospital of Paris (1856), Professor of Pathological Anatomy at the University of Paris (1872). A position of Professor of the diseases of the nervous system was specially created for him. He established the neurology clinic in 1882. Classical French Neurology was founded by him.

He would work uninterruptedly into the night and was a prolific writer. He articles regularly appeared in Lancet and BMJ. He also authored many books. He was a popular teacher and his students came from all over Europe. He adopted theatrical techniques and lectures to teach the students. His famous students included Babinski, Bechterew, Pierre Marie, Freud, and Bouchard, Bornville.

Bouchard was one of his good students. Bouchard being egoistic felt that he should get equal glory if not more for their joint activities - Charcot- Bouchard aneurysms was an example of this. Bouchard felt very neglected because his name came after that of Charcot!

He was the teacher of Babinski. Babinski was thought to succeed him. Unfortunately for the crucial selection examination, Charcot could not come and Bouchard replaced him as the chairman. Babinski was not selected and it changed his life completely. He became very famous but never became a teacher officially.

His contribution to the understanding of Multiple Sclerosis and differentiating it from Paralysis Agitans was then considered outstanding. He was a clinical wizard and was variously nicknamed as the 'Napoleon of the Neurosis' and 'Caesar of Salpetriere'.

His 18 eponymous contributions include - Charcot -Leyden crystals seen in the stools of patients with

Amoebiasis and the sputum of patients with asthma; Charcot's (Neuropathic) joint seen in leprosy, diabetes, Tabes dorsalis, syringomyelia - a non inflammatory hypermobile painless joint; Charcot - Neumann crystals in semen; Charcot's (cerebral) triad - Nystagmus, Intention tremor, staccato speech seen in Multiple sclerosis; Charcot's(Biliary) triad - Right upper quadrant pain, Jaundice, intermittent fever in cholangitis. Charcot's artery of cerebral Haemorrhage - Lenticulo striate branch of MCA; Charcot - Bouchard aneurysms - aneurysms of the perforating branches of MCA which can result in cerebral haemorrhage.;

Charcot's edema - a painful edema seen in hysterical paralysis; Charcot's disease or Charcot's sclerosis -Lou Gehrig's disease a rare disease from which the baseball player of that name died; Charcot - Marie - Tooth disease - Peroneal muscular atrophy; Charcot's hysterogenic zones; Charcot - Wilbrand syndrome - Visual agnosia due to PCA occlusion; Erb - Charcot paralysis - a rare from of spinal syphilis; Charcot's angina cruris - Intermittent claudication; Charcot - Jeffroy syndrome of epidural ascending spinal paralysis.

His pastime was music and Beethoven was his favorite composer. In 1882, University of Wurzberg honored him with a doctorate. He started to get attacks of angina pectoris and his health deteriorated. He died in 1893 of pulmonary edema at Morvan in France. His famous quote included "symptoms then, are in reality nothing but cry from suffering organs". and "to learn how to treat a disease one must learn how to recognize it. The diagnosis is the best trump in the scheme of treatment". So true!

THE STORY OF ASCLEPIUS - THE MAN WHO COULD BRING THE DEAD MEN BACK TO LIFE - WHY WAS HE NOT IMMORTAL?

According to the Greek mythology, Asclepius could bring the dead back to life! This was probably his undoing. What is known about his life history makes an incredible story.

His birth was indeed controversial and interesting. His mother was Coronis from Trikala of Thessaly. She had a secret affair with Ischys. When Apollo learnt of this, he wanted to kill her. On his command, his sister Artemis killed her on the funeral pyre. While watching this, Apollo felt guilty of killing the unborn innocent baby and rescued it by splitting open the womb - probably the first recorded caesarean section in he history of mankind! He adopted this baby as his own and brought it up under the mentorship of half human half horse Chiron a famous for his medical skills. Thus Asclepius learnt his medical skills from Chiron.

He became a very successful healer with exceptional medical skills. He mastered the art of surgery and the art of medicine including the use of drugs and aphrodisiacs. He is supposed to have given Gorgon blood with magical properties to Athena. Gorgons had snakes for hair, bronze claws, wings and eyes that could turn humans into stones. The blood from left side of Gorgon would kill a man and that from the right side would bring back a man from death.

Asclepions were built in his honor and memory after his death. The famous Hippocrates studied medicine from one such Asclepion on the Kos island and started his medical career there. One should also note that the original Hippocratic oath mentions the names of Asclepius and his daughter Hygea (goddess of hygiene) and Panacea (goddess of universal remedies). His 2 sons were Machaon and Podalarius who were great surgeons. They healed a 10 year old wound of an archer Philoctetes who later raised the bow to kill Peris to end the decade long Trojan war.

However, the Asclepion, a rod with a single serpent wound around it is more famous than Asclepius. This signifies his exceptional skills in treating snake bites. It became the symbol of doctors and modern medicine should not be confused with Caducius a staff with 2 snakes intertwined which is more a symbol of occult art carried by Hermis when he carried the souls from the land of living to the land of the dead.

Because of the incredible powers of Asclepius, many who were supposed to die did not die. Hades, the god of dead complained to Zeus the god of skies who in turn struck Asclepius with a thunderbolt and killed him. Asclepius, his staff and the serpent became a constellation in the sky.

Even Bible mentions that Moses during the exodus out of Egypt wandering in wilderness in search of the Promised Land raised a serpent made of copper on his staff like the rod of Asclepius, called Nehushtan. Mere looking upon it was supposed to heal people with snakebite! Snakes were regarded to have great healing powers and non poisonous ones were left free in the dormitories where the sick lived. The snakes were believed to rejuvenate themselves by shedding their skin and therefore were believed to cure the sick!

DIFFICULTY IN UNDERSTANDING THE SUBJECTS IN THE FIRST YEAR MBBS - WAS IT EVERYBODY'S PROBLEM OR WAS IT MINE ALONE?

I write books. Mainly medical books. It is my passion. I am at home communicating with the reader. I feel that it is the right of the reader to know the subject better and the responsibility of the author to present the matter intelligently and intelligibly.

When I joined MBBS, I was horrified to see the books let alone reading them. I never imagined their size and complexity. I asked my friends about this. All of them said they also found it difficult. Of course, there were exceptions. There was this Australian student who claimed to be able to understand and recite the complicated textbook of Physiology by Samson Wright (We called it Samson Wrong because we could not make head or tail of it!). I did not believe him till he gave me a demo - he could recite the page verbatim. he went one step further he started telling the last words in each line correctly! Spellbound and depressed I asked him for the secret of this memory. He promised to tell me after the vacation after the first sessional exam (6 months after joining). He went home to Australia and never returned.

My next stop was a senior Professor who was a very good teacher. He was very impressive. He invited questions - no one dared to ask. He would always recommend Physiology textbook by Best and Taylor and explicitly tell us not to read a much simpler Indian book by Chatterjee. One day I ventured into his chamber. I was indeed surprised to see this! I asked him why was he reading the book that he specifically did not want us to. Imagine my surprise at the answer he gave -" to find out the source of your mistakes" was the answer!

Anatomy had to be studied from Grey's textbook. It was voluminous with very small letters. I was wondering why some letters are even thinner and some slanting. Much later I realized that these changes that I perceived were due to my Astigmatism - printing was perfect! That is when I began to look fr other books - Grant's for Diagrams, Hollinshed for color illustrations, Sahana for 'distilled version of Gray', a book for embryology and one for the mnemonics. Cunningham Manual for dissection was a must and we had to refer 11th edition. With all that the subject was tough. The trick was to memorize a fund of otherwise useless information. As one of my then classmates put it, Physiology was" mugging with reasoning" and "anatomy was mugging without reasoning"! But mug all had to do to pass the subjects. Repeating these would be a sure prescription for insanity.

Biochemistry was the smallest of all the subjects - in fact it was not even an independent subject - a small part of Physiology. It was the easiest to understand but very difficult to remember. One would get the feeling of mastery after one round of reading. Try to remember the facts, and one would remember almost nothing!

That's when I learnt what 'volatile subject' meant! Just as a volatile substance which easily evaporates and eventually leaves no trace of the substance, the knowledge of biochemistry particularly the cycles 'evaporated' leaving no trace of any material one had carefully read and studied! It was a torture to remember the cycles and phenomena. Practical exams was a different ball game. One of the experiments where perfection was needed was a 'titration' experiment. There was a lecturer who would say add half a drop more - till the end I never figured out how one could add half a drop - when the drop for a drop forming will always be a full drop!

Towards the latter part of the first MBBS course lasting for one and a half years, I started liking Physiology immensely. Maybe that was the prime reason for my taking up Medicine as my career later. My fear for Anatomy later became less but I could not imagine a career in the same! But I still admire some of my teachers - particularly one who was ambidextrous who later migrated to the US and became an anesthetist!

After the one and a half year course, there was an examination - one of the most dreaded - and most of us were fortunate to clear it - I say fortunate because the pass rate was one in 3! We moved over to the clinical side where we saw live patients. This was a welcome change. We felt very happy. Soon we realised that there was no real escape from the basic 3 subjects that we had just passed. They continued to follow us. Even now we need them! Only solace is that we do not have to appear for the exam again!

FOOTPATH IN MANGALORE - A MYTH OR REALITY? - IS THERE ANY FOOTPATH LEFT?

Footpath is a self explanatory term - a passage specially created for the safety and convenience of the pedestrians. I vividly remember walking on quiet and the safe footpaths of Mangalore as a young boy accompanying my mother to the market.

What has happened now? Many roads just do not have footpath. The basics insist that when a road is created, road, drains and footpath have to be constructed as a unit. Earlier there was not much of technology - but there was robust common sense. Now there is modern technology and no sense common or uncommon!

If by chance the road you chose to walk on does have a FOOTPATH what has happened to it? Food vendors occupy it in the plum places parking their carts - making it a FOODPATH. People crowd round it effectively blocking what is left of it!

Many ladies walk on the road and therefore the flower vendors are sure to occupy a corner making it a FLOWERPATH. Many varieties will be available in a small space!

Vendors of footwear are ubiquitous and there is no better place than the footpath to sell them - they convert the footpath into the FOOTWEARPATH!

Autos and 2 wheelers and sometimes 4 wheelers are parked on it as if the owners of these vehicles also own the footpath making it a FOOTPARK!

Some self respecting people are upset and try to tell the vendors that they are blocking the path and being an obstacle. If looks they give could kill, these guys would surely be dead - making it a MURDERPATH!

Come elections, or festivals the footpaths now will be occupied by the poles and banners - usually holes are dug into the footpath to stabilize the banners - a sure way to destroy it permanently!

Once I remember reaching the venue at Bangalore late when I was an invited faculty for a lecture for a Post Graduate Medical Education Programme because the road was blocked for some drama festival!

Is there any remedy for this problem? Probably the change has to come from within. Common sense and civic sense have to be rediscovered. After all the footpath is primarily meant for the pedestrians.

I only hope that these people who usurp the footpath realize their fallacy and vacate the same it will again be a pleasure to walk safely on the footpath. Let us rediscover the joy of using the footpath properly

THE LAST WORD

$\mathbf{W}$ay back in 1970, when my headmaster, Mr. Anantha Rama Rao Verkady summoned me to his room, I was surprised. It was to tell me that I was one of the recipients of the national merit scholarship for having figured in the list of first 100 ranks in the state SSLC examination. My joy knew no bounds. He gave me a letter to that effect and another accompanying letter to be signed by my father, a physician, and indicated where my father had to sign it. The scholarship was a prestigious one and would look after my education till my Phd if ever I chose to do it! When I proudly gave the letter to my father he was extremely happy. He went through the contents of the letter very carefully and appreciated my achievement but flatly refused to sign it.

He pointed out to me that an income limit was prescribed and that his income exceeded that limit marginally. I tried to convince him by saying that by signing this he would be absolved of all responsibilities of my entire education. I however failed miserably in my efforts.

I then put forth my last argument saying that if he did not sign the letter for his son, the next in line would sign it for his own even if his income exceeded the prescribed limit. To this my father coldly replied "that is the difference between his father and your father!" Needless to say I never received the said scholarship but only Rs. 100 as a token and a certificate instead. This action of his reflected his honesty, transparency and discipline.

The day before his demise, when he was unable to swallow, I politely suggested that he may be admitted into a hospital and be given intravenous fluids. I felt that I was doing what was best for him as he always did for me. But he refused the suggestion immediately. The speed of decision and the finality of his voice reminded me of the incidence in school.

The voice however had become feeble, but the spirit had not diminished. Needless to add, as usual, he had the final say in the matter!

THE CASE OF THE "WRONG CALL"

It was a very tiring day. I went to bed at about 11 45 and slept off immediately. I had to get up at 4 45 next day to be able to go to the gym. At about 12 15 I was woken up by the shrill ringing of my mobile phone. I picked up the call almost immediately

The caller, obviously a lady was inconsolably crying. I was surprised but all the same decided to continue the call as the caller was obviously in distress. After a while of sobbing and actual crying, the caller introduced herself as a PG in Pediatrics. A baby had died in the ICU of her institution and the relatives were threatening to manhandle her and her co PG both ladies in the first year of training. Obviously it was the wrong call. I am heading the department of Medicine at a different institution. The first thought was to say so and softly encourage her to call her HOD. I asked her whether the higher authorities have been informed. She replied saying that she tried to but they refused to take any responsibility saying that only imparting education was their responsibility. I immediately understood the seriousness of the situation. I surmised that the person must have saved the number as HOD and dialed it. Still it beat me why she dialed me! By the time she realized that I was not the person she wanted to speak to and promptly disconnected. I tried calling her back and she did not pick the call.

I like mysteries - I always liked to read the novels based on mystery. I always thought that the problem can be solved by logical thinking and action. Now I got an opportunity to put these into action. The number, name of the caller and the institution were the only leads available. Were they enough to solve the puzzle at the dead of the night? Was I justified in helping a PG from another institution? I have 2 daughters who are doing their higher medical training at different institutes. I would have appreciated someone going out of the way to help them. Then I should also do the same!

I had to do some quick thinking. Maximum number of the seats this time went to PG s from Andhra. So, logically no harm thinking that this girl is also from Andhra. I have always found PG s from Andhra quite resourceful and closely knit. So I decided t wake up an Andhra PG and gave him the number and name of the PG and the institution. To the credit of all Andhra boys, they tracked the identity of the person in next 15 minutes! The phone belonged to one of the PG s from our institutes who had stored my number as HOD. He gave the phone to his wife who was working in that institution and in turn, she had lent it to her friend during the hours of duty. This solved the mystery why she had called me.

Then came the appropriate action. The PG whose wife was having the mobile went to the spot. He was surprised by what he saw. The ladies were hiding inside a small room in ICU. There was a commotion outside the ICU. It was pathetic to see that the management security or the police did not take it seriously. The doctor who went successfully escorted the lady PG s out of the ICU and took them to a safe place.

This case is another eye opener. Do we have to wait for something to happen before helping the ladies in distress? Where is the chivalry? It is nauseating to see the people not even doing their own duty for which they are regularly paid. I feel only making people liable for their inaction will be a good answer. There should be stiff fines based on the duration of inaction. Repeated offences should lead to successive demotions and dismissal altogether after the last possible demotion.

THE EPISODE OF THE MAN WHO SWOONED

I reach the HOD office of Medicine department at 9 AM. today as usual. After meeting the people, signing documents and dictating a few letters and communicating digitally with some people I was driving to the teaching hospital.

A narrow road leads to the hospital. Usually vehicles are parked on the left side of the road and that makes the road even narrower. To make the matters worse, some two wheelers come on this narrow one way road from the opposite side. This forces the pedestrian to walk virtually in the middle of the road exposing himself to all the vehicles. A car stopped. An elderly man got out of the car and even before closed the door, swooned and fell. Another car passed him and possibly grazed his head. I was 2 cars behind this and saw it happen. As it was an unexpected event and there were people around, I was not too sure whether the man's head was hit by the door or the car that passed. The man who fell down started to bleed from his forehead just above the right eye. I was in 2 minds. I parked the car on the side of the road, got down came to that car and watched. The man driving that car also was an elderly man. He was shaken by the episode. People gathered around and started to ask questions. "What is the color and make of the car that passed by?" asked one person. He blamed the driver for not noting the number. The driver was trying to put the man inside the car into the back seat and was struggling to do so. No one of the 50 or so people gathered around helped. One scooterist came from the opposite direction and blocked the door to ask some stupid questions of gossip value. He had to be shooed away to make way for the patient to be put inside the car. I helped the old man to do this. Then I volunteered to accompany them to a hospital leaving my car behind. I left the hospital only after making sure that the person was stable and his daughter arrived.

Whatever happened to our civic sense? Why do we hesitate to help people in distress? Is it the reflection of "me" attitude rather than "we"? Maybe like the nuclear family. We are distancing ourselves from serious problems - "As long as it is not me why should I bother" is one reason. "Why should I get involved in a police case?" is the other one. How on earth do we expect these people to help us in our crisis?

By helping them I got delayed elsewhere. I do not know whether I am right or the other 'wise' people are right. I am sure there are more questions than answers. Sometimes the answers may be obvious and sometimes the answers may not come at all.

I suddenly remembered my childhood days when we were a big homogeneous group unconditionally helping each other. If a boy fell from a tree and got injured, we would stop playing, attend to him, give him water, take him to the nearest doctor who usually did not charge, get medicines take him home and tell only the mother (underplaying the seriousness) and avoid the father and disappear. We pledged to remain so for all time to come and help each other and other people also. I wonder whatever happened to the pledge!

THE SWEET MEMORIES OF VISIT TO A MOVIE THEATRE

The day on which all of us were taken to a movie in a theater was a big day. It was a family outing much looked forward to. It was a rare occasion and had its own special appeal. As a young boy maybe in the early primary school, I remember accompanying my dad to a classic - «Benhur». I was awed by the war scenes and the seriousness of the movie what if I understood nothing! The settings were great and I thought that the war scene was real! also remember going to some Hindi movies with my mother and aunt. The dressed worn by the actress were displayed in the theater. I understood nothing of the hindi movies but felt very bad when almost every one cried in the theater! The movies I really enjoyed were the Kannda movies with Narasimha Raju a comedian playing some role usually with Raj Kumar. I was so fond of him that on a trip to Bangalore when my aunt, a doctor at Bowring Hospital asked me what

I would like to visit most in Bangalore I replied "Of course, Narasimha Raju!" She politely told me she did not even know where he stayed and I tried to convince her that maybe he lived on the road they had just named after him! This was during my 7 th standard vacations. Any movie would begin with a "News Reel" a black and white depiction of news. One of the news surely would be about "Rashtrapathi Radhakrishnan". For some reason the black and white news played much faster than natural. I was really impressed by the 'speed' of the old politicians till I later understood that it is a technical problem!

In the school they would rarely show us some excellent black and white movies. Usually they were about some scientific discoveries or about rockets, space travel etc. I would eagerly wait for that rare day. I still remember some scenes from those movies clearly. My beloved uncle would take us (my cousin and myself) to some English movies at the New Chitra talkies. Usually they were spy movies. Enemy was always more intelligent than what the hero assumed him to be. However after all the action (usually mindless - ending in a large factory which produced God knows what) the hero always won convincingly! This was during the high school, PUC and MBBS days. During the Post Graduation I would go to movies with my friend Gurudutt who was studying to be an Ophthalmologist. We would see an English movie on most Fridays. It would cost us Rs. 3.50 each for the balcony ticket (in the front portion). Reaching the theater from the hospital would cost less than a rupee. One packet of Masala ground nut and a cold drink each would be around Rs 2. So Rs. 10 in all saw us through a movie session. We walked home after the movie which was healthy and free.

I just cannot come to terms with the present day scenario of going to a movie theater. Gone are the days of cheap tickets and simple eats. You are forced to take a huge packet of popcorn and a big coke. Some times one wonders whether people go there to eat or t watch the movie. Movies themselves are insipid. They are made by the people with questionable IQ s for people with even lower IQ s. Rarely we find gems among the muck. 100 crore club probably is another social club like Rotary or Lions nothing to do with the actual collections! However there are no superstars any more. No wonder people do not take the trouble of visiting movie theatres regularly. Any 3 Hindi movies seen in the course of 1 year will give you material and ideas sufficient for that year's releases. Once in a way however, a Lunch Box, a Dirty Movie, a Kahani will surface keeping the hope alive and faith intact. No wonder we hardly remember recent movies and never forget the movies like Lawrence of Arabia, Titanic, Inferno, and the like!

THIS IS NO MONKEY "BUSINESS"

We (my wife Shobha and me) are just back from a trip to Malaysia and Bali. We were specifically told to watch sunset at Uluwatu at Bali. On the last day of our trip to Bali we planned this after checking out of the hotel before reaching the airport.

There are 2 things to see at Uluwatu - an old Shiva temple for which the entry is highly restricted. There is a specific dress code which we were not aware of and so we could not enter the temple as such. Then however, there was the sunset to watch and it can be watched from many points. You get a good view of the ocean too.

There are many monkeys at Uluwatu. In fact they are encouraged and pampered. There is an exclusive swimming pool for the monkeys - something I have not seen anywhere. And there are very many monkeys. One can sit and relax in the benches provided from where the sunset is not visible. One could watch from the edge of the wall but it is not possible to sit there. We were sitting on one of the open benches when we met a family of 3 French ladies 2 sisters and their mother. The mother had a bandage on her little finger. On inquiry, she revealed that the injury was due to the monkey attempting successfully to snatch a banana in her hand. In the process he scratched and bit the little finger. She had to visit a hospital meant for the foreign tourists and was given a shot of tetanus toxoid and one of ARV. The whole thing cost her a whopping 100 $! The monkey's prank turned out to be expensive indeed!

As the sun set was approaching, I called my wife to stand near the wall so that the sunset can be viewed better. She did so. She was busy talking to me and the people around us. Then she moved back to the open benches saying that there is still more time. 2 guides belonging to 2 other groups were sitting beside her on both sides. Just then in one swift move she felt her glasses being snatched from her face suddenly. Before she could realize it was a monkey, he fled with the glasses and sat above the wall near which I was standing. On the other side of the wall below the spot where the monkey was sitting, there was the ocean in full glory. There was a patch of grass just beside the wall where I was standing.

The monkey carrying the Cartier glasses which indeed was an expensive gift, jumped up and sat exactly above me and started to examine the glasses. My wife was desperate as there was no way we could reach the monkey and get the glasses back. There was very little time and little we could do. I was about to shout at the monkey when a local man advised me to remain calm. He gave the monkey a small chocolate in his right hand. The monkey gladly took the chocolate, for a while held the chocolate in his right hand

and the glasses in the left hand and examine both. He must have found the chocolate more interesting and therefore threw the glasses down and was busy eating the chocolate. Now came the second hurdle. The glasses fell down into the patch of grass behind which was a cliff leading to the ocean. There was no way we could reach the spot where the glasses lay. The same man helped again. He jumped the wall and in one swift move retrieved the glasses and jumped back to safety and returned the glasses to us. The whole thing was so sudden that we were stunned. Even before we could recover and thank him or offer him a gift, the man had vanished. All along, a Chinese tourist was video recording thwe whole thing and he had his dark glasses on his forehead. The monkey came back and in one swift move removed his dark glasses, jumped up to the same high spot, turned round the gasses, had a good look cut it into 2 parts and sincerely gave one part back to the gentleman and threw the other part into the ocean. The glasses were destroyed forever.

I shudder to think what would have happened if that fate had befallen my wife's glasses. In fact, my heart was beating in my mouth when the monkey was examining the glasses. It was a stroke of good luck that the unknown gentleman came along and helped us. My only regret was that we could not thank him properly.

Need I say that we immediately proceeded to the airport without caring to watch the sunset. We proceeded to the airport in a taxi driven by Made Yasa who by then had become our friend. I made fun of my wife all along the way. We reached the airport, completed the security formalities and I found a newspaper and settled down to read it as there was time for departure. That is when I realized that my glasses with the case were missing. Obviously, the monkey had taken it even without my knowledge! I am not too sure who had the last laugh - my wife or the monkey!